MOUNT ROYAL COLLEGE

D0621166

Date Due

MOUNT ROYAL COLLEGE
LIBRARY

BUILD YOUR
CUSTOMER STRATEGY

BUILD YOUR CUSTOMER STRATEGY

A GUIDE TO CREATING PROFITABLE CUSTOMER RELATIONSHIPS

JAMES G. BARNES

WILEY

John Wiley & Sons, Inc.

This book is printed on acid-free paper. ∞

Copyright © 2006 by Barnes Marketing Associates, Inc. All rights reserved.

Published by John Wiley & Sons, Inc., Hoboken, New Jersey.

Published simultaneously in Canada.

No part of this publication may be reproduced, stored in a retrieval system, or transmitted in any form or by any means, electronic, mechanical, photocopying, recording, scanning, or otherwise, except as permitted under Section 107 or 108 of the 1976 United States Copyright Act, without either the prior written permission of the Publisher, or authorization through payment of the appropriate per-copy fee to the Copyright Clearance Center, Inc., 222 Rosewood Drive, Danvers, MA 01923, 978-750-8400, fax 978-646-8600, or on the web at www.copyright.com. Requests to the Publisher for permission should be addressed to the Permissions Department, John Wiley & Sons, Inc., 111 River Street, Hoboken, NJ 07030, 201-748-6011, fax 201-748-6008, or online at http://www.wiley.com/go/permissions.

Limit of Liability/Disclaimer of Warranty: While the publisher and author have used their best efforts in preparing this book, they make no representations or warranties with respect to the accuracy or completeness of the contents of this book and specifically disclaim any implied warranties of merchantability or fitness for a particular purpose. No warranty may be created or extended by sales representatives or written sales materials. The advice and strategies contained herein may not be suitable for your situation. You should consult with a professional where appropriate. Neither the publisher nor author shall be liable for any loss of profit or any other commercial damages, including but not limited to special, incidental, consequential, or other damages.

For general information on our other products and services, or technical support, please contact our Customer Care Department within the United States at 800-762-2974, outside the United States at 317-572-3993 or fax 317-572-4002.

Wiley also publishes its books in a variety of electronic formats. Some content that appears in print may not be available in electronic books.

For more information about Wiley products, visit our Web site at http://www.wiley.com.

Library of Congress Cataloging-in-Publication Data:

Barnes, James G.
  Build your customer strategy: a guide to creating
profitable customer relationships / James G. Barnes.
    p.   cm.
  Includes index.
  ISBN-13: 978-0-471-77660-4 (cloth)
  ISBN-10: 0-471-77660-2 (cloth)
    1. Customer relations.   I. Title.
HF5414.5.B36825   2006
658.8'12 — dc22

                                                          2006008676

Printed in the United States of America

10 9 8 7 6 5 4 3 2 1

ACKNOWLEDGMENTS

In many ways, this project is based on lessons that I have learned over many years of talking with the customers of hundreds of companies. I am a firm believer that listening to customers must form the basis for company success. If we fail to treat customers well and give them what they want, they will leave—simple as that! I have tried in this book to gather my thoughts on what works and what doesn't, from the customer's perspective. I am indebted to the many hundreds of customers with whom I have talked in person and who have been surveyed on my behalf. Without their candid feedback, I would have been unable to compile this guide to customer strategy.

Many people have contributed advice, ideas, and feedback along the way, some of them consciously and others merely by allowing me to be in their presence and to learn from them.

I am fortunate to be associated with the CRMguru.com organization, and thank Bob Thompson for the opportunity he provides for me to communicate with the worldwide membership and with my colleagues on the Guru Panel. I particularly have welcomed the insight of Paul Greenberg, Naras Eechambadi, Graham Hill, David Rance, and Mei Lin Fung and the editorial guidance of Gwynne Young.

I have also benefited from my association with the team at 180 Solutions, Inc, where Brian Vallis and Grant Lee have provided me the opportunity to meet and interact with hundreds of small and medium businesses. Through 180 Solutions and affiliated companies in Australia and the United Kingdom, I have been fortunate to work closely with the most talented group of individuals with whom I have ever been associated. I thank Anthony Mitchell, Jackie Furey, Ross Smith, Colin Coverdale, Ian Waddelow, and Robert O'Dowd for the opportunity to work with them and for sharing their wisdom with me and the amazing Peter Silver for his technological wizardry.

Others have directly and indirectly contributed to allowing me to refine and test my thinking and my customer strategy model. In particular, I thank Leigh Puddester, Belinda Sadlowski, Mike Mielnichuk, John Gardner, Brian Lewis, and Heather Tulk for providing me the opportunity to work with them and their companies.

I have benefited immensely from the insight of my friend and colleague, Bruce Hunter, who has served as a willing sounding board for many of my ideas and provided candid feedback. Martha Rogers offered advice along the way that I greatly appreciate. I thank Gary Gorman of Memorial University for his ongoing support and Mykila Sherren for producing the graphics.

As always, my colleagues at Bristol Group continue to contribute to my learning and to opportunities to work with wonderful individuals and clients. My thanks go especially to Rick Emberley, Brian Cull, Gloria Robbins, and David Ryan.

I am delighted to be working with the professional editorial team at John Wiley & Sons, and particularly thank Sheck Cho, Helen Cho, Natasha Wolfe, and Julie Burden.

Natalie Slawinski worked very closely with me in developing the framework for the book, in clarifying and refining some of the more complex concepts, and in challenging me where needed. Her contribution and commitment were invaluable.

I dedicate this book to my family, and especially to Diane, who continues to indulge my passion for customers and who regularly helps me see things that I miss.

2006   JIM BARNES

CONTENTS

INTRODUCTION

WHERE'S YOUR CUSTOMER HAT?

Why is it that just about every business executive and manager you meet will proudly tell you that their company is customer focused, yet, when you talk with their customers, you are met with violent disagreement?

I have spent more than 30 years listening—listening to the experts in marketing and customer service, your customers. In the past few years, one important thing has become very obvious to me: Customers are now way ahead of the companies that are trying to woo them. Customers know what they want, they know where to go for information, and they are supremely confident in their ability to make decisions that will be best for *them*. I'm not sure they were ever comfortable being sold at, but it is very obvious now that customers don't want to be merely the *target* of selling efforts on the part of firms that are mainly interested in achieving their own goals.

This book will help you develop and implement your customer strategy: the strategy that must be in place before you can compete effectively in today's complex world. But before you begin to put your customer strategy together, you have to commit to wearing your customer hat to work.

Not only have too few executives taken the step to develop a customer strategy, but many seem decidedly uncomfortable wearing their customer hats to the office. This is a metaphor that I believe addresses an intriguing phenomenon. Most managers have little difficulty regaling family, friends, or colleagues about their own experiences with various businesses and can clearly express their feelings toward those firms when things go surprisingly well or horribly wrong. Yet those same managers often seem oblivious to the fact that their own customers may be experiencing the same kinds of feelings. What is it about that customer hat? Why is it so hard to take it off the hook and put it on when we get to the office?

Just about every executive one meets today has also bought in to the notion that companies, if they are to be successful in the long term, must build customer relationships and loyalty. But surprisingly few have a deep understanding of what relationships and loyalty really entail. These are emotional concepts, but most firms think of them in behavioral terms: If they come back to buy from us again and again, they must be loyal and we must have a relationship with them. Wrong! My purpose in writing this book is to challenge you to develop an emotional connection with your customers; and you will need a strategy to get there.

It's Not a Marketing Strategy

The pendulum has well and truly swung. The model under which companies have interacted with their customers for the past 50 years or so is no longer valid. It is no longer sensible to delegate responsibility for the customer to the marketing department or to any other department. There has been so much change in the customer's environment in recent years that conventional approaches have been rendered practically obsolete. If your company continues to behave toward your customers as you did even a couple of years ago, you are in danger of being left behind.

There has been a long-standing assumption in many companies that marketing owns the customer. This may have been appropriate thinking 30 years ago, but it is certainly not appropriate today. One of the most important conclusions that I can draw from my conversations with customers of many companies is that *an overwhelming portion of the factors that drive long-term customer satisfaction and decisions about whether to come back and buy again lie outside the conventional responsibilities of the marketing department.* Great products at great prices simply don't cut it any more.

I'm not the first to make such an observation—no less an authority than Jim Stengel, global marketing officer of Procter & Gamble, observed in an often-quoted speech to the American Association of Advertising Agencies in 2004 that the existing marketing model is obsolete—and this is a message that you will hear many times in the years ahead. Companies have to change the way they deal with their customers if they have any hope of reaching that elusive grail of genuine customer loyalty.

Larger firms in particular are well equipped with strategies that they will pull out at the drop of a hat. They will proudly display their growth and product development strategies, their advertising and communications strategies, their pricing and distribution strategies, many of which are based on very costly marketing research. But what some companies are now reluctantly admitting is they lack a customer strategy—a strategy to guide how they deal with and treat their customers, how they communicate with them (or, more correctly, at them), what experiences they create for them, and ultimately how they make them feel.

This book is not about helping you develop or improve your marketing strategy. It's much broader than that. It's not about helping you sell more stuff this week. It's about building a genuine connection with your customers so that they'll want to do business with you well into the future, will bring in their friends and associates, and will even be prepared to pay more for what you have to offer—because it's worth it!

The Hard and the Soft

The world in which larger companies in particular operate today is very much characterized by a focus on the "hard side"—a world dominated by data and by a striving for short-term financial results. The organizational tendency that governs most company behavior is to gravitate to the functional rather than the emotional—the hard rather than the soft.

This is a recurring theme in this book: Managers and executives must realize that there is a critically important soft side to what they offer their customers and to how they interact with them. Many companies have spent many millions of dollars on customer relationship management (CRM) systems in an attempt to get closer to their customers and to build relationships. But CRM as technology is simply more hard-side thinking. It's approaching the creation of relationships as defined by the firm, not by its customers.

In fact, I have often wondered, if we were to survey the customers of some companies that have implemented CRM, whether those customers would have noticed any difference as a result of that implementation; whether they would feel better treated, more comfortable, or even proud of the firms; whether their emotional connection would be any stronger than it was before the companies spent all that money on CRM.

The main reason that CRM often is unlikely to lead to stronger, emotionally driven customer relationships is that the CRM thrust of the firm is often initiated without a clear strategy. In a survey of its worldwide membership in late 2005, CRMguru.com found that more than 60 percent of those responding indicated that their greatest need is for information on how to develop a strategy to guide CRM in their firms.[1] The next most frequently mentioned need was for content on how to create a customer-centric culture.

Customers don't think like companies, they think like people. They are inclined toward the soft side. Companies, and their executives and managers, tend to think and behave like hard-side companies. It is this company-think that makes it impossible for some of them to wear their customer hats around the office.

They look for shortcuts. They look to other firms to provide them with "best practices." But each company and each customer interaction is unique. You have to make your own best practices. The creation of your best practices will be driven by a deep insight into the hearts and minds of your customers and of what they want when they deal with you.

If you are to truly understand your customers and the opportunity that exists, you will need to *complicate* things a little, to better understand some of the softer concepts that are so important in building that customer connection. The management literature is full of references to concepts that appear extremely useful in developing a customer strategy—value, customer relationships, expectations, customer experience, and so on. But, while many firms can produce documents and plans that are replete with such references, there is scant evidence to suggest that there has been much depth of thinking devoted to understanding how to use them to advantage. When we have superficial understanding, we have superficial application.

There must be less simplification and more complication. Managers need to think more deeply about the concepts that form integral components of the customer strategy. There is a tendency to take the easy way out; but this is human behavior and human emotions that we are dealing with here. These are not simple processes or concepts. We have to understand them deeply.

Technology: The Double-Edged Sword

I am inclined to blame technology for the organization tendency toward the hard side. There is simply far more data available today—at very low cost, by the way—than management has had in the past. Data are automatically captured at virtually every transaction and customer touch point. Executives have become enamored of and totally reliant on data, to the point where it has replaced deeper customer insight in many firms. Because we have the data, it is easier to identify inefficiency and to focus on optimizing marketing spend. The outcome has been that many companies treat customers as data points and not as real people. They exist only as records in a database. This attitude *depersonalizes*; it contributes to the antithesis of a relationship.

Yet that same technology has brought power to your customers and has made it infinitely more difficult for you to reach them. They get the information they need from the Internet and from blogs, and pay less and less attention to mass media messages. So you need a different solution from conventional marketing. You need a strategy that leads to the establishment of that emotional connection, because, at the end of the day, your customers are people with innate human needs. They want to be treated like people, not like numbers in a database.

Commitment, Not Campaign

At the same time that I see phenomenal change in the way that customers view and function in this new world, I see much less acknowledgment of the magnitude of that change among executives than there should be. Many firms, even if they do see what is going on, seem to have little appetite to make the changes necessary to respond.

In this book, you will be challenged to change how you think about customers and behave toward them. You will need more empathy and sensitivity in your company, and you will need to be a lot more creative in terms of how you conduct yourselves in dealing with your customers. You will have to be prepared to break out of that famous box inside which we have all been accused of thinking.

One of the most important messages I want to leave you with deals with the importance of listening. I'm surprised how many executives I meet spend little if any time actually engaging their customers in conversation. Yet every customer has many, many stories about the companies with which he or she deals and delights in telling them. Listen to their stories. They contain exactly the gems of insight that you need to build your customer strategy. You need a greater understanding of customers, what they are going through, what they are trying to accomplish, and what role you and your company and its products and services can play in their success.

What Lies Ahead

This book is intended to change your company by changing how you, your management team, and your employees think about customers. It will challenge you to look at the world through their eyes, with your customer hat on. It will certainly challenge you to think more deeply about some concepts that you may have been using to describe and refer to customers in the past.

We begin in Chapter 1 by discussing in depth some of the points that I have made briefly in this introduction, encouraging a broad-based view of the customer and of the building of relationships. In Chapter 2, we challenge the importance of customer satisfaction in the building of relationships and introduce a five-level framework for understanding how genuine relationships are formed. Chapter 3 explores value as the essential component of relationships and makes the critical distinction between functional and emotional forms of value.

Chapter 4 asks how your company or brand can come to mean something special to customers, how meaning can be created through the building of an emotional connection. Chapter 5 establishes the importance of customer experience in making that connection, but suggests that there are many forms and levels of experience that can be utilized, each creating progressively more emotional value. Chapter 6 delves deeply into the highest form of customer experience—the experience that your firm can create or enhance for your customers.

Chapter 7 explains what's at stake, what you stand to gain if you succeed in building an effective customer strategy, debunking the conventional view of what "loyal" customers are worth. Chapter 8 reiterates the need for deep customer insight to guide strategy development and for a different approach to measurement to determine how successful you have been. Chapter 9 is a guide for your management team on what it will take to build and implement your customer strategy, what's likely to get in the way and how to achieve buy-in and encourage creativity.

We end in Chapter 10 with a step-by-step guide for building the customer strategy, complete with a template that you and your colleagues can follow in building your own customer strategy.

Thanks for joining us on this exciting departure from the conventional and for having the confidence to go back to the basic principle of starting with your customers to build your strategy for the future of your firm.

Endnote

1. CRMguru.com, Member Survey, 2005.

1

HOW DO YOU MAKE THEM FEEL?

During a recent focus group project, the subject of shopping was explored—a topic that is easy for women to talk about, but about which most men have little to say. The discussion was animated and enthusiastic. The women who were participating talked about how they "love" to shop at certain stores, how they can't wait to see what they'll find, the "thrill of the hunt," the "get-away-from-it-all" feeling when shopping with a friend, the fact that a "nice lunch" is an integral part of the ideal shopping trip.

All of this led to the obvious conclusion that shopping, at least for many people, is an emotion-filled experience. Sure, there are aspects of shopping that are viewed as a chore—something that I have to do—but, for the most part, *real* shopping is enjoyable. And many women have their favorite stores—places they go back to over and over again, where they feel welcome, and where the staff "knows them," does them small favors, and offers great advice.

A discussion in one group of young mothers was absolutely fascinating. They talked longingly about how they shopped before the kids came along and how they miss it. They commented about how their lives are completely taken up with their children and how shopping today is all about the kids. Tracy, who was quiet for a few minutes, obviously thinking, made a most important observation when prompted. She said, "You know, when we become mothers, we often forget we are women."

This is the kind of insight that is critical if companies are to deal with their customers in a way that will build solid relationships. It's precisely the kind of information on which customer strategies can be built. Tracy was presenting an opportunity for retailers to address. How can a retailer help a young mother who is preoccupied with her children recover some of the enjoyment of shopping and the feeling that she matters? The retailer who cracks that issue and behaves differently toward this target segment will become much more than a retail store in the minds of Tracy and her friends.

THE FOCUS IS ON THE CUSTOMER—JUST LISTEN!

You need to know how your customers feel about doing business with you, whether there is any hint of something approaching a relationship. This book will reflect your customers' view of what it means to them to be dealing with your firm or buying and using your brand. To provide you with that perspective, I will draw on more than 30 years experience listening to customers from a wide variety of industries, both end consumers and business customers, in several countries. I have always believed that, if companies would only listen more closely to their customers, they would have a far easier job satisfying them and building loyalty.

Customers are very vocal in discussing businesses with which they have dealt or tried to deal. Think about how often your conversations with friends, family members, and colleagues at the office turn to experiences with businesses: how long you had to wait to be served, the great deal you got yesterday, or how the sales associates "couldn't do enough for you." Customers are prepared to tell us what they like and what they don't, what works and what doesn't, what will cause them to go back, and what leads to a decision never to deal with you again. If we would only listen to the words they use and the feeling in their voices, the road to building solid customer relationships would be a lot simpler.

In this book, I will share with you the insight that I have gleaned from my conversations with customers. In many ways, I'll be speaking on behalf of *your* customers, interpreting for you how they feel about dealing with companies like yours. We will listen to their words, their comments, and their reactions to situations that they encounter in dealing with businesses both large and small.

There is no doubt in my mind that many firms are able to develop long-standing, genuine relationships with their customers. We see it all the time. There are many examples in your own life where you keep going back to the same companies, not only because they offer great products at great prices, but often because you *feel* welcome when you enter the store or because you *feel* comfortable dealing with the staff.

But don't go looking to your customers to comment on their *relationships* with you and your brand. In fact, it is interesting that customers will rarely use the R-word when talking about their dealings with companies or their purchase of particular brands. It seems that many would consider it a weakness on their part if they were to admit to having a "relationship" with a supermarket or a bottle of ketchup. Yet customers will regularly drive past three or four supermarkets to get to their "regular" one and will ignore two or three lower-priced brands of ketchup in order to buy Heinz.

It is this appreciation for an emotional connection between customers and their favorite companies and brands that will preoccupy us in this book. We will explore how customers develop genuine relationships with companies and brands, and will set out to show managers and executives how such relationships can and must be developed in the interest of long-term business success.

ARE YOU CUSTOMER FOCUSED?

When I speak to groups of businesspeople, I often ask how many would describe their companies as customer focused. With the exception of a small number who are either painfully honest or embarrassed, usually 90 percent or more will say that they are. In fact, it's fashionable today to position one's company as customer focused or customer centric. Few executives will admit that they aren't focused on customers.

But, when we dig more deeply into what executives mean when they describe their firms as customer focused, we find that many take a decidedly *company-focused* view. Their view of the customer extends to collecting as much data as possible, so that better-targeted offers can be placed directly into the real or electronic mailboxes of precisely those who will respond to them. This view of the world is indeed focused on the customer, but with the goal of selling her more stuff and in the most efficient way possible. A CEO recently asked me if I could devise a strategy that would see his firm deal *only* with its most profitable customers. This is a decidedly short-term view of the customer, one driven by monthly sales quotas and quarterly profit targets.

My approach in this book is to focus much more on the cultivation of *long-term* genuine relationships with customers, relationships that will withstand the competitive overtures of companies that are seeking short-term sales results driven by campaigns and special offers. This relationship-based approach is different. It challenges executives to think differently about their customers, to truly understand what it means *from the customer's perspective* to have a relationship with a company or brand. It means that you must not only accept the solid logic for developing long-term customer relationships, but that you also must understand why it is a good idea, and what it means to customers to have a relationship with your firm. As we will see in Chapter 7, the payback from such an approach is potentially enormous.

Unfortunately, many firms seem not to understand or accept this logic. As customers ourselves, you and I continue to encounter businesses that frustrate us, make it difficult to deal with them, obviously do not understand what we are trying to accomplish, and generally disappoint. Yet many suggest that it is common sense that, if we treat people well, they will likely come back and buy from us again. They may even tell their friends and colleagues in one of those business-focused conversations how much they enjoy dealing with us. If it is so commonsensical, it certainly doesn't show in many companies. This book will challenge those companies to think differently about their customers, to understand what it means to be truly customer focused.

WEAR THAT CUSTOMER HAT

I meet businesspeople in social or other nonbusiness settings who often have stories to tell about an experience they have had with a retail store, or a hotel, or a local dry cleaner, and will regale those listening with their account of what happened and how they now feel about the company in question and how they will never go back and are mystified at how companies could behave like that! Yet if we were to do the research with their own customers, we would find at least as much disgruntlement and dismay among their customers at how their company could be so insensitive as to treat them like that.

What's happening there? I regularly encounter situations where businesspeople with whom I deal, themselves passionately involved customers, ready to criticize other firms, seem to be blinkered when it comes to how their own firms are behaving. They seem to leave their customer hats at home when they go to the office in the morning. They get to work and immediately start thinking like businesses rather than thinking like people. They don't seem to be able to make the link between their own experiences as customers and how their customers may be feeling and talking about their firm.

A LONG-TERM STRATEGY

One of the most important factors that gets in the way of a relationships-focused view of the world, particularly in large, publicly traded companies, is the fixation on short-term financial results and on tangible, revenue-producing assets. Many companies seem to spend little time thinking about where future revenues and profits are likely to come from. It seems rather obvious to me that a company should act to protect the stream of earnings that are driven by those customers who are loyal to the company and will continue to bring in business over many years. Yet customers are often treated like short-term revenue-generating machines, with little thought to the much greater profits they have the potential to produce 5 and 10 years ahead.

The customer relationships that a company is able to cultivate represent the most important asset that will *never* appear on its balance sheet. As such, companies need to develop strategies for the management of that extremely valuable asset, which, because of its intangibility, is difficult for many to really understand. Often managers have difficulty with such a "fuzzy" concept. They are much more comfortable managing things that can be and are measured. As a result, most companies that I meet have no customer strategy in place. Many take an extremely short-term and shortsighted view of customers—bordering in many cases on an attitude of "What have you done for me lately?"

A more positive view is to realize the potential that lies in solid, long-lasting customer relationships and then to develop a strategy that will create them and sustain them. Companies that design and implement such customer strategies will gain an advantage over competitors and will reap the long-term benefits, as we will discuss in much greater detail in Chapter 7. Customers notice when companies are *genuinely* interested in them, when they truly appreciate their business and are sincerely committed to their satisfaction. They also know when the relationship is one-sided, when the company is "only trying to sell me something." Customers are increasingly less comfortable being sold at and are much more inclined to deal with firms where they are treated as if they matter.

WHEN IS A RELATIONSHIP A RELATIONSHIP?

The answer to this question is easy. It's not a real customer relationship until the customer *feels* that it is one. I am intrigued by the fact that some companies believe that *they* can decide to establish a relationship with customers, or that they have a relationship merely because customers come back to buy again or because the customers are members of the "loyalty" program (which has little or nothing to do with loyalty, by the way). I have listened to enough customers over many years to realize that they will, over time, develop an emotional connection with certain companies and brands. These will come to *mean* something special to their customers and will constitute that stable set of firms and brands upon which those customers will come to rely. They will use very personal language in describing their favorites and will actually take a certain degree of ownership.

Loyal customers will refer to "my supermarket" or "my shampoo" in much the same way that they will refer to "my doctor" or "my hairdresser." I have seen regular customers of airlines, hotels, and retail stores quietly take an employee aside when they have noticed something wrong to suggest that the employee may want to take corrective action before someone else notices. The unspoken (or possibly spoken) comment is that "This is my company too and I expect better of us."

The same phenomenon is obvious when customers attach nicknames to their favorite companies, stores or brands. Generations of Britons have bought their undies at "Marks & Sparks." Regular shoppers of Target Stores refer to their store as "Tar-Jay," imbuing it with a cachet of Euro-fashion feel. In Canada, a very large percentage of the population will know exactly where to go if a friend suggests they meet at "Tim's" for a coffee, because the Tim Hortons chain has succeeded in becoming such an integral part of the Canadian social fabric.

I firmly believe that only relationships that *customers* perceive to be special constitute solid long-lasting assets for the firm. I make an important distinction, therefore, between customer relationships that I describe as genuine and those that are superficial or artificial. For a customer to be truly loyal, and for a relationship to be genuine, there has to be an emotional connection. The relationship has to be *meaningful,* in the sense that the firm or brand must come to mean something special, to be seen to occupy a meaningful place in the life of the customer.

If you are thinking right now that this is unlikely or at best a remote possibility, let me suggest that the vast majority of customers with whom I talk regularly will speak with a great deal of feeling about how disappointed they are when a favorite brand changes its formula so that it becomes "new and improved," how much they miss it when a favorite restaurant closes, and how they dread having to "break in" a new banker when their personal banking officer is transferred to another city.

One customer described her favorite supermarket to me as "home away from home" because she felt so *comfortable* there. It is powerful emotional attachments such as these that drive behavior. Customers go back again and again to those companies and brands that feel special to them and that make them feel special. We all have such companies and brands in our lives. The challenge is to understand how they got to be that way.

One technique that I often use to encourage executives to think about how they might achieve the status of genuine relationship with their clients or customers is to get them thinking about what they would ideally want their customers to be saying to friends or colleagues about the firm or its products a year or two from now. The more functionally focused managers will suggest that they would like their customers to be saying things like "they have great _____ there" or "I always know I'll get the best deal at _____." The problem is that such answers relate to products and prices, and great relationships are based on much more than these.

I would want my customers to be saying things like: "I don't know what I would have done without them," "Thank goodness they were there," and "I know I can always count on them to _____." Such comments from customers reflect the emotional attachment I have been talking about. The question is how we achieve a situation where such comments can be heard in customer conversations across the country. Executives need to work backward to strategize on what will have to happen for customers to offer such comments. This process will begin to give us some insight into what we have to do and how we have to *behave* as a company to develop that attachment on the part of customers.

THE HARD AND THE SOFT

I have come to the conclusion that there is a "hard" side and a "soft" side to marketing and to what companies offer their customers. We'll return to the theme of hard and soft throughout this book, as it is a central component to relationship thinking. Simply put, the hard side of the offer to customers or the firm's value proposition consists of the things a company *must* do if it is to be considered a serious competitor. It's the quality and variety of its products, the prices it charges, the efficiency of its distribution system, its accessibility to customers, and the technology that supports much of what the company offers.

The soft side of the offer, however, is much more about how the company conducts itself, how it behaves toward its customers, and how it treats them. It's more than the efficiency of customer service; it's about how the company and its people interact with customers, how they deal with them, and ultimately how customers are made to feel as a result. This is indeed a more "fuzzy" side of what companies offer, and it is often difficult for executives to appreciate and act on, accustomed as they are to the more tangible and measurable side of the business.

I firmly believe and regularly observe that most managers, if left to their own devices, will gravitate to the hard side when seeking a way to enhance their offer to customers or in an attempt to increase customer satisfaction. I further believe, based on my conversations with customers, that the soft side is much more important to customers in determining whether they develop that genuine relationship that we have been discussing. Increasingly, customers take the hard side for granted; they *expect* companies to get the functional and product side right—these are less and less of a differentiator as product and service quality improves and technology increasingly enhances efficiency. I can usually get most managers to grudgingly admit that their competitors have pretty good products too, that their distribution systems are actually quite efficient, and even their prices represent good value for money.

The hard and soft issue is one that very much gets in the way of companies becoming more customer relationship focused. It's really about the classic right-brain and left-brain debate. The culture that exists in most companies, the reward systems that are in place, corporate goals and objectives, all encourage a left-brain focus—an emphasis on the analytical, rational, tangible things that can be most easily conceptualized, measured, and managed. The problem is that, in many companies, this emphasis impairs the organization's ability to think about the things that are likely to truly impress customers and lead to that emotional connection.

Do customers want companies to get the hard things right? Of course they do! But are these things sufficient to create a meaningful experience or to impress the customer to the point that she will tell her friends? Probably not. At the end of the day, the customer is more impressed with the softer things, the right-brain thinking, the pleasant surprises, the obvious understanding, the employees who seem to genuinely care, the phone call that is quickly returned.

CUSTOMERS ARE PEOPLE, NOT DATA POINTS

It is fashionable to suggest that customers have changed, that they are much more sophisticated, more knowledgeable and demanding, more fickle. Some even suggest that customer loyalty is dead, that customers are less likely today to establish relationships with companies and brands. I'm not at all sure that this is the case. What *is* obvious is that the *environment* in which customers live and function today bears scant resemblance to that to which their parents were exposed. One doesn't even have to go back a generation to see what phenomenal change has occurred, particularly in technology and the competitive landscape.

There is no need to go into detail here on how the marketplace has changed. There is a lot more competition—and therefore choice—than ever before, and that competition comes not from the guy down the street but from companies operating from other countries, thousands of miles away. Customers are faced with a mesmerizing array of choices in brands, in retail stores, and in how to buy. And, of course, technology has changed everything, from how and where we listen to music, to when and where we do our banking, to how we buy a new BMW or a used King Cobra 6-iron.[1]

Customers are potentially better informed than ever before, but it is more difficult for marketers to reach them with their messages. They have more choice in what to buy, where to buy it, and where to learn about it. In most product categories, customers are going to the Internet in search of often less-biased information before going out to buy. Word of mouth has become word of *mouse,* as consumers engage in the electronic swapping of product information with people they will never meet face to face. At the same time, media fragmentation is making it much more difficult to reach customers through the mass media and driving marketers to below-the-line vehicles such as sponsorships, direct marketing, and product placement in an effort to get their brand and their message in front of prospective customers.

The product-quality issue has largely been beaten through a combination of advancing technology, government- and industry-imposed standards, and the sheer competitiveness of the marketplace. It's virtually impossible for a company to survive today if its products are inferior.

Technology has probably had the most important impact on changing completely the environment in which consumers operate. It allows companies to be much more impressive today than ever before in how they interact with and serve customers. FedEx will get your package to Seattle by 10:30 tomorrow morning and will allow you to track its progress online. Lands' End will allow you to "try on" a new outfit in the privacy of your personal virtual dressing room. eBay connects the world in an international garage sale *cum* auction that is founded on trust and a sense of community.

But despite this tremendous change in the environment to which both business customers and end consumers are exposed, and the resultant changes in behavior that have been brought about, I would argue that, as people, customers haven't really changed very much at all. At the end of the day, they are impressed with the same things, they want good value, and they do not want to be disappointed or frustrated. Despite the obvious changes in the retail environment, women still state exactly as they did 10 or 15 years ago that, when they go shopping, they want to feel relaxed, not rushed or pushed to buy something; they like to be pleasantly surprised; and they enjoy shopping with a friend and having lunch at a "nice" restaurant. These are fundamental human needs or desires that are unlikely to change, even though the physical world may have changed dramatically.

The environment has witnessed spectacular change and customer behavior has changed in response, but people are still people. Some want to save money and buy at the lowest price. Some want to buy online and to complete their transactions as painlessly and conveniently as possible. But one of the universal truths in marketing is that there are segments in every market and in every company's business. Many customers actually *want* more personal service and are prepared to pay more. I regularly encounter customers who tell me that they would gladly pay *more* "if the company would only _____."

If companies and their executives would stop and think about how their customers would like to feel when dealing with them and what they *really* want from businesses, they would realize that customers generally want to feel important, noticed, recognized, and appreciated. They prefer not to experience situations that will make them feel angry, frustrated, or let down. As obvious as this seems, it's equally obvious that many companies fail to deliver consistently.

One problem that gets in the way of understanding how to create the most conducive setting and experience for customers is that many companies treat them not as people with unique needs, challenges, and situations but rather as data points. Some managers tend to view customers as data to be analyzed rather than people to be understood. Although many larger companies in particular have become especially skilled at data collection and data capture, and have extremely detailed databases filled with the most minute information about their customers, for the most part the data tell us about the customers and what they have bought, but little if anything about why or about who these people are.

Changes in the environment and in the marketplace have prompted changes in customer behavior and have made it easier for customers to switch and to walk away—all the more reason why it is important for firms to appeal to their emotions so they'll put down roots.

WE NEED MORE INSIGHT, NOT MORE DATA

Despite the fact that a database reveals that a customer bought several bottles of fine Bordeaux, or flew to New York last month, or called a particular phone number 12 times last week, it isn't really a very personal source of information about customers. Just because my VISA card record shows that I bought two dozen white roses, it will never reveal for whom and for what occasion. The phone company's database may show that I called France 12 times last week, and will even indicate the number called, but it will never be able to say why. The problem with databases, regardless of their great level of accuracy, is that they are not at all good at digging deeply into the *context* in which the customer is operating. We buy things and make calls and visit stores for reasons that are personal to us. To do a better job of serving their customers and to achieve the desired level of customer relationship, companies need a great deal of insight into the lives and circumstances of their customers, not more data.

REMEMBER THAT QUARTER-INCH DRILL

We as marketing executives need to know a great deal more than is commonly captured in customer databases if we are to address some of the more deeply held needs and wants of customers. Believe it or not, customers don't really *need* what we are selling. As Harvard professor Ted Levitt famously observed, "No one goes out to buy a quarter-inch drill; they need a quarter-inch hole." In other words, they need the results that may be obtained through the use or consumption of the product. It is also the case that a competitor's product may serve the purpose equally well. So we need to find reasons for the customer to fly our airline, or visit our store, or ship with our courier company. We need to be able to tap into needs that the customer may not even be able to identify and verbalize.

Only by obtaining the necessary insight can executives begin to formulate the customer strategy that's needed. Strategy is, by definition, based on solid information—that's what being strategic means. There is a logical progression from data to insight.[2] While data will tell you what customers bought, it is typically historic, numeric or financial, and limited to what we are able to capture through scanners, card swipes, and other systems. Once data are analyzed, companies extract information that allows them to identify patterns and correlations in the data that are useful for directing marketing initiatives.

But none of these sources will produce the kind of insight that's needed for firms to respond to unvoiced customer needs, to identify opportunities to impress customers by doing the unexpected, by identifying situations that the customer would not expect us to address. This is, again, a recurring theme in this book—think back to Tracy at the beginning of this chapter. Companies, if they are to establish meaningful relationships with a large number of their customers, should be constantly on the lookout for opportunities to surprise and impress customers by behaving in ways their customers would never expect.

THE LITTLE THINGS AREN'T — LITTLE, THAT IS

Companies often overlook the little things. Yet they have the potential to derail a customer relationship. In the retailing project that we talked about at the beginning of this chapter, we asked what would cause customers to leave a store without buying or earlier than they had planned. No surprise to me, the answers indicated that the likelihood of staying in a store had less to do with product selection and price than it did with how "comfortable" shoppers felt.

We heard a great deal about "little things" that surface as irritants for the customer and are often ignored by retailers. Much was made of the appearance and feel of washrooms and about such details as the use of single-ply toilet tissue — customers think it's cheap and shows the retailer doesn't really care. Several women said they would never buy clothing in a store where the mirrors are *outside* the changing rooms. They were quite vocal about how they feel "parading themselves" in public wearing something that may not fit and they may not buy.

Tracy probably does not expect a retailer to make it possible for her to enjoy a shopping day with a friend, without the kids. But wouldn't she be impressed if one retailer rose to that challenge? Wouldn't she and her friends think better of a retailer that used two-ply or even three-ply toilet tissue in the washrooms (and maybe even had fresh flowers!), or one who had the mirrors (and lots of clothes hooks!) *inside* the changing rooms, and maybe even provided coloring books or toys to amuse the kids while Mom tried on a new sundress?

To reach the stage where such initiatives become a conscious part of a company's strategy, the firm must first have a culture that accepts that such things can make a difference and also must have the kind of insight that is needed to drive such action. Without an intimate understanding of what goes through the customer's mind, we can never formulate a strategy that will impress her. The better the information, the better the strategy.

NOT MARKETING AS WE'VE KNOWN IT

In many companies, it is suggested that the marketing department owns the customer, that anything that relates to interaction with or directing initiatives toward the customer is the logical responsibility of marketing. But many companies also take a very shortsighted view of what marketing is all about. In such firms, marketing is responsible for the marketing mix but is not really responsible for the customer. In my experience, much of what contributes to the satisfaction and loyalty of customers lies outside the boundaries of conventional marketing. Customers often go back to their favorite retail stores because they are known by specific salespeople who have been "looking after them" for years. Conversely, many more refuse to deal with a firm again because of some "little thing" that happened, something that is often far removed from the responsibilities of marketing. I suspect that marketing departments are typically not responsible for the quality of toilet paper in the washrooms, yet that detail may send female shoppers home early.

Many firms have not evolved very far from the sales-driven stage that characterized the 1960s and is immortalized by stereotypical salespeople. They are very sales oriented in that much of the marketing effort involves short-term campaigns intended to produce short-term sales results. They employ sales personnel, pay commissions, and offer incentives that are designed solely to sell things. There is much emphasis on price, which encourages a sizable segment of customers to shop around for the lowest prices. In fact, the influence of discounters, led in most markets by Wal-Mart, has created a mind-set that one should never pay full price for anything. The result is the "butterfly customer" who is seen to flit from one retailer to another in search of the lowest prices. But this butterfly did not emerge from its cocoon on its own; it is a creation of a marketing/retailing mentality that seems to think that everyone wants to pay the lowest price. They don't.

A customer strategy is an anti–price-competition strategy. My research with clients has proven time and time again that those customers with the strongest relationships are prepared to pay *higher* prices in order to deal with their preferred companies. They will often observe, "I know I'm paying more, but it's worth it to me." It all comes down to the perception of value, a subject that is discussed in Chapter 3. A customer strategy is a value-creation strategy and is not reliant on the conventional tools in the marketing tool kit. It means that we have to either bolt on a customer strategy to the existing marketing strategy of the firm, or we need to extend the boundaries of what we refer to as marketing in order to accommodate this emphasis on building long-term relationships with customers.

It is becoming progressively more difficult today to compete on the basis of the marketing mix as it has been defined for the past 50 years. In most industries, product quality has improved and most competitors are doing a pretty good job; the product has become commoditized. Price is extremely competitive, and it's futile to go head to head with the price leaders. Distribution is efficient; delivery is overnight; access is 24/7. Communication is fragmented and increasingly controlled by the customer, not the firm. Marketing in the future will have to involve less sell and more serve; less push and more pull; less tell and more listen. Competition is tough, especially in the absence of a customer strategy to guide the development of relationships.

IT'S ALSO A DIFFERENT VIEW OF CRM

In the past 10 years or so, CRM (customer relationship management) has burst on the scene mainly in the form of software systems that are intended to make the company's contact with its customers more efficient and to create high levels of customer satisfaction and retention—satisfaction mainly with the hard side, I might add.

But CRM is not simply software or the application of technology. CRM is also the culture of the company; a culture that appreciates that customer relationships, if they are to be genuine and not simply repeat buying behavior, must be grounded in an emotional connection with the company or brand. In many firms, especially those that feel that their investment in CRM technology has been poorly spent, the assumption was that CRM software would create more solid customer relationships. Actually, what most firms wanted were higher rates of customer retention and more profitable customers.

You would be right to ask at this point "Isn't that what all companies want?" And I would answer that it is indeed, but it is not enough. Why settle for mere retention, if you can achieve relationships? Why settle for short-term sales, if you can cultivate an army of committed, loyal customers who will guarantee you a steam of earnings well into the future?

The view of CRM as software misses the point that all forms of software are simply tools that enable the achievement of certain objectives. As Rigby, Reichheld, and Schefter pointed out in the *Harvard Business Review,* one of the greatest pitfalls of CRM programs as they have been implemented in many companies is that the companies bought and installed the software before putting a customer strategy in place.[3]

My view is that a technology-based approach to CRM is simply not sufficient for a company to achieve genuine customer relationships. There must exist a parallel view of CRM as culture, as an abiding perspective within the firm. Before a company can hope to develop long-lasting relationships with its customers, it must know them intimately, it must also have a collective mind-set that reflects a genuine commitment to the customer and to addressing a wide range of customer needs. This means that the firm has to think and behave in a way that customers will notice. I'm not sure how many customers notice when a company invests millions in CRM software.

In many companies, CRM has been adopted as a new way of doing business because of its promises to make marketing initiatives more efficient, to allow companies to direct their marketing initiatives to customers who are most likely to buy, to equip call centers with immediate information from client files to allow for higher levels of cross-selling and up-selling, to allow the firm to reduce marketing spend directed to less profitable customers. In short, it's all about us, about our success and efficiency. It's not about the customer, really, except insofar as we'll be able to sell her more stuff. It's really an extension of the sales-driven school of marketing. It perpetuates a depersonalizing view of marketing as something we do to customers.

In fact, CRM-driven initiatives that result in better-targeted direct mail, cross-selling efforts every time we talk to a company, and less attention being paid to "underperforming" customers may well have a counterproductive effect. It's a form of *CRM paradox*. The customer contact that is driven by the CRM program results in better-targeted direct mail going to customers who don't want to receive it, up-selling initiatives being directed at customers who don't like being sold to, and some customers who have been extremely loyal actually getting *less* attention from the firm and feeling neglected as a result. The outcome of implementing this form of customer relationship management program may well be weakened relationships, not stronger ones.

THIS ISN'T NEW, BUT IT'S NOT EASY EITHER

The way of thinking about the customer that represents the thrust of this book is not new. Small businesses have been doing it for generations. But they are in the best position to get to know their customers and to deliver personalized service—two of the building blocks of customer relationships. The challenge is to turn what comes naturally for many small firms into a strategy that can be implemented in much larger organizations.

In the chapters that follow, we will explore the process of developing and sustaining relationships that customers will agree represent something special, that establish a connection with the customer that results in more than mere repeat buying. We will talk about how companies must create emotional value if the customer is ever going to feel a certain connection with a firm or brand. We will discuss how relationships can be meaningful and how we can achieve the lofty status where customers will actually be *proud* to be *your* customers.

We will take some of the mystery out of creating a great customer *experience*, something that everyone seems to be talking about these days, by showing you how you can approach the customer experience in ways your competitors haven't even thought of. We will talk about managing difficult relationships, such as those that take place via technology or at great distances, and those that are in danger of going off the rails.

We'll show you how you can actually take the pulse of the relationships you have with segments of your customers and identify where those relationships are weak and where they are strong. And we'll give you a template so that you can develop your own customer strategy, using the building blocks of successful relationships that are presented at the end of the book.

Thanks for joining us in our quest to build meaningful customer relationships. We are confident that your company will be more profitable and more respected well into the future as a result.

Endnotes

1. For an excellent overview of just what has changed in the environment of the customer, see a special report entitled "Crowned at Last: A Survey of Consumer Power" in *The Economist,* April 2, 2005.
2. James G. Barnes, "The Role of Customer Insight in Building Your CRM Strategy," a CustomerThink white paper, published by CRMguru.com, 2003.
3. Darrell K. Rigby, Frederick F. Reichheld, and Phil Schefter, "Avoid the Four Perils of CRM," *Harvard Business Review* 80, no. 2 (February 2002): 101–109.

2

ARE THEY LOYAL OR MERELY SATISFIED?

Let's clear up some confusion: Is it loyal customers you want, or merely satisfied ones? There is a big difference, so I would opt for as many loyal ones as you can get, if I were you.

Producing satisfied customers should be relatively easy; all you have to do is get most things right and generally do what customers expect of you. If you can accomplish this, chances are you'll regularly get 8s and 9s on your 10-point customer satisfaction survey. I'd suggest that, if you're not scoring 8s and 9s, then you have some serious problems. If you can't get scores approaching 10, then this means that you are regularly disappointing customers. If you disappoint them with any degree of regularity, the chance of developing a close relationship is pretty slim.

So let's not confuse satisfaction and loyalty: Satisfied customers are not necessarily loyal, but loyal customers are almost certainly satisfied. I say "almost" because it is possible for very loyal customers to be dissatisfied with an interaction or a component of your service and still remain loyal. In fact, that's one of the benefits of creating loyal customers; you can disappoint them every now and then and they will still remain loyal.

Now, while we're at it, let's clarify the distinction between two other terms that are often confused. Retention is not a relationship. Retention is a behavioral concept, while relationship is an emotional one. Retention means that a customer comes back to buy again; a relationship means that she has an emotional attachment to the company or brand. High levels of retention are good but vulnerable. Strong customer relationships are better and much less vulnerable.

GREAT EXPECTATIONS

Customers enter purchase situations with certain expectations—it doesn't matter if they are business-to-business (B2B) customers or end consumers.

Whether buying office equipment or a tennis racket, raw materials or sushi, attending a sales conference or a Willie Nelson concert, customers have ideas about how they want to feel during the purchase process and while they are using or experiencing the product or service. Customer expectations are based on prior experiences in similar situations, on what advertising and other forms of communications have promised or implied, and on what the customer feels ought to happen. They serve as a reference point against which the actual experience of dealing with a firm is compared, consciously or subconsciously, leading to the customer being relatively satisfied or dissatisfied.

For the most part, customer expectations are predictable; that is, customers expect the product to be of a certain quality, to be delivered on time, to find all the parts in the box, and to represent good value for money. They also expect to receive polite and prompt service. Firms that can meet most of their customers' predictable expectations can generally achieve fairly high levels of customer satisfaction, but they may never achieve loyalty.

We expect customers to be able to express their expectations, that they are consciously aware of them. Also, when we speak of customer expectations, we are most often referring to expectations about the *level or quality of products and service* that we provide. In other words, when businesses address the concept of customer expectations, it is usually in the context of what customers generally expect firms such as ours to do. We don't usually address the question of what new and different things customers might find appealing but really don't expect us to do.

My research indicates that customers' expectations are very much bounded by the context in which they are operating: namely, their interaction with a firm that operates in a certain industry. In other words, their expectations are based to a large extent on what they would typically expect a company to do in this situation. Customers expect products to be in stock. They expect to be served in a reasonable time and that they will have phone calls and e-mails returned. They expect deliveries to arrive when promised, that the quality of products will be acceptable, and that staff will be generally knowledgeable and friendly. For the most part, their conscious expectations rarely go beyond the predictable components of what they expect us to do.

THEY DO NOT EXPECT TO BE SURPRISED

By definition, customers do not expect the unexpected—they do not *expect* to be surprised. Therefore, when service either exceeds or falls short of what customers consider acceptable, they experience satisfaction or dissatisfaction. Thus, the generally acknowledged way to impress customers and to contribute to satisfaction is to at least meet expectations relating to the quality of the product or service.

But customers also hold a set of expectations that are subconscious, that are activated only when certain events occur. These are passive expectations that are not usually thought of because they have become permanently encoded into the customer's view of the firm. We don't even think about the mundane or commonplace—of course McDonald's will have fries; of course Avis will have cars available. We take such things for granted. Such expectations do not become important until they have been exceeded or dashed; that is, after the interaction with the firm occurs—an employee goes out of his way to please, or we find that there are no cars available. It is these sub-surface expectations that contribute to an outer range of customer emotions that may result from the interaction with the firm, to emotions as extreme as delight and disgust.

SATISFACTION IS FUNCTIONAL, LOYALTY IS EMOTIONAL

Satisfaction is achieved to the extent that your company can meet your customers' conscious expectations. If you ask them what they expect from you, they will tell you quite predictable things relating primarily to the *functional* side of the value proposition. Creating satisfied customers, reaching 9s and 10s on that customer satisfaction survey, is quite simple; all you have to do is meet those rather basic and predictable expectations. If you get everything right that they expect of you, they'll be satisfied. And keeping them satisfied will get them back again. By doing things right, you will create higher levels of retention.

But achieving customer loyalty is a different proposition. Loyalty comes through the creation of an emotional connection. Satisfaction is a step along the way. The emotional connection is based to a very large extent on a firm's ability to exceed those expectations that customers are unable to verbalize, that reside in the subconscious. It takes surprise and delight to make an emotional impression on customers. They have to be impressed to the point where they thank you and gush, "I didn't expect you to do that for me." They aren't impressed with the fact that Office Depot has copier paper in stock or that Publix has enough checkout lanes open, but they will be frustrated, disappointed or even angry if they don't.

SATISFACTION IS PERSONAL AND SITUATIONAL

What satisfies one customer may not satisfy another; in fact what satisfies a customer in one situation may not satisfy that same customer in a different situation. Much of what contributes to a customer's level of satisfaction in a certain situation is internally driven. We can't separate satisfaction from the customer. Whether you succeed in satisfying a customer is influenced very much by the situation in which the customer finds herself—her expectations, her mood, her desired outcomes. At best, you and your employees can anticipate what's needed; you can't control the situation.

Think, for example, of eating in a restaurant. Say you and a colleague from your office decide to grab a quick lunch today at a restaurant down the street. You are probably on a fairly tight schedule—you want to get back to the office for that 2:00 P.M. meeting. Over lunch you discuss the proposal that is due on Friday. It's a business lunch, and you want certain things from the restaurant and its staff. The most important factors that will influence your satisfaction are the speed and efficiency of the staff and the service. If things don't move quickly, you become frustrated and even angry.

Now, fast forward to Saturday evening. You have booked a table at the same restaurant to celebrate your partner's birthday. What are your expectations and needs on this occasion? It's the same restaurant and the same you. But the circumstances are completely different. On this occasion, speed of service (within reasonable limits) is not that important. In fact, if you are hurried through the meal and are finished within an hour, you feel rushed and disappointed. This is a much more relaxed setting, and it takes quite different service and treatment to achieve customer satisfaction.

Knowing what satisfies each and every customer can be an impossible task. Some of the factors that contribute to customer satisfaction are "no-brainers"; you have to get these right even to be considered competitive. In many industries, core product and service now fall into that category. The bar has been raised so high that customers expect products that rarely, if ever, fail. Things that were considered valuable additions to the core offer just a few years ago are now standard procedures and expected of everyone. A good example is getting your car washed when you bring it to the dealer for service. Ten years or more ago, if you got your car back and it had been washed, you were impressed. Today, at least where I live, most dealers will wash your car before you get it back. It's no longer a big deal. In fact, if they *don't* wash your car today, you are disappointed. Bars get raised.

FRAGILITY OF CUSTOMER SATISFACTION

Mere satisfaction is not enough. If we are not careful, scoring 8 or higher on customer satisfaction will lead us to believe that things are okay, that we've got a loyal group of customers. Frederick Reichheld is generally acknowledged to have pioneered the thinking that even satisfied customers will leave if a better offer comes along. He showed in his research that between 65 and 85 percent of customers who switched suppliers were satisfied or very satisfied prior to their departure. His conclusion: "Current satisfaction measurement systems are simply not designed to provide insight into how many customers stay loyal to the company and for how long."[1]

For some reason, companies seem to be focused on scoring at least 8 out of 10 on customer satisfaction. When they achieve this magic number, there is widespread cheering and backslapping. I think it may have something to do with the fact that, in North America at least, in schools and colleges 80 percent is an A. If you achieved an A in school, you were doing very well. We all want to be A performers.

My research in the financial services, retail, and telecommunications industries on both sides of the Atlantic demonstrates conclusively that customers who score 10 on the 10-point satisfaction scale (i.e., those who might be labeled "completely satisfied"), as compared with those who score 8 or 9 (i.e., those I have labeled "merely satisfied"), give firms considerably more of their business in the category ("share of wallet"), and are much more likely to indicate that they plan to remain customers and to recommend the firm to friends and associates.

I am convinced that, when asked how satisfied they are, customers' minds turn again to the predictable things they associate with the provision of the products and services that we sell. We compound the issue by asking them predictable questions about how satisfied they are with the quality of the product, whether they were served promptly, and whether the staff thanked them. Such measures of satisfaction are driven more by short-term functional factors because that's what comes to the customer's mind when he or she is asked about satisfaction. Few think more deeply about the more emotional connection with the company. That's why we can score 8 or 9 and still be vulnerable to competitive activity that lures customers away.

The company's view, equally, tends to be focused on product and service quality, on price and the service interaction. This is what managers think drives satisfaction, and it does, but only satisfaction with the immediate, transactional aspects of the customer connection. Thus a customer may be pleased with the fact that she was served quickly, that he was able to get into and out of the store in five minutes, that the flight departed and arrived on time. But this says little of how the customer actually feels about the company.

BRIDGING SATISFACTION AND LOYALTY

Achieving high levels of customer satisfaction on short-term transactional measures is important, but such satisfaction is vulnerable unless accompanied by a longer-lasting, more deeply held connection to the company. As soon as a competitor comes along who can do it better, faster, or cheaper, customer satisfaction dissipates and becomes irrelevant. In the absence of an emotional bond, the customer will eventually leave.

Measuring customer satisfaction is important and firms should be encouraged to capture such information, but its limitations should also be recognized. Unless the firm is also measuring those things that drive satisfaction and customers' more deeply held attitudes and emotions, it runs the risk of being lulled into a false sense of security when it comes to the loyalty of its customers. The firm may be confusing satisfaction with loyalty.

The point is that customer satisfaction is an extremely important step along the road to developing solid customer relationships, but that in and of itself satisfaction will not lead to relationships. We must not only meet customer expectations around predictable things, but we must also exceed their expectations about things they do not expect us to do. Surprising customers will impress them and begin to create an emotional connection. This represents the basis for loyalty and a relationship.

IT'S NOT A RELATIONSHIP, BUT I *LOVE* SHOPPING THERE!

Many consumers feel uncomfortable talking about *loyalty* when the term is applied to businesses or brands, probably for the same reason that they will express discomfort at the suggestion that they may have a *relationship* with a company or brand. Words like *loyalty* and *relationship* are reserved to describe our interactions with other people, principally family and friends. To suggest such intimacy with corporate entities or inanimate objects is discomforting to many.

In fact, of course, consumers do develop loyalties to both companies and brands. They develop strong, long-lasting relationships that see them going back willingly time after time. They come to *rely* on companies, to *trust* them, and to feel *comfortable* doing business with them. Brands become a defining part of the consumer's persona; they take on importance and meaning. If there was ever any doubt about the existence of brand loyalty and relationships, it is dispelled in a wonderful article by Susan Fournier, written in 1998, in which she describes in vivid detail conversations with ordinary consumers about the products that they use in their daily lives, brands that truly mean something special to them.[2]

LOYALTY IS ALIVE AND VERY WELL

As mentioned briefly in Chapter 1, some authors and commentators on modern society have decreed that loyalty is dead. They point to an increasingly fickle consumer, bombarded on all sides by advertising and an amazing variety of products and services. Couple this with the ease of switching brought about by advances in technology, the accessibility afforded by the Internet and the extremely competitive marketplace, and it is *de rigueur* to think of consumers flitting from brand to brand, company to company, with little thought of developing anything approaching loyalty.

But this is a supply-side view of what's going on in the lives of customers, a view that focuses on changes in the marketplace, not what's going on in the minds of customers themselves. I am convinced that customer loyalty is alive and well. There exists a natural human need to develop loyalties, not only to friends and family, but to organizations and to brands. What is not working well in many companies is an appreciation for how to create genuine loyalty.

What role does loyalty play in the lives of customers? A very large percentage of consumers have an innate desire to develop loyalties, to put down roots. They go back again and again to companies where they are treated well and where they feel "comfortable"—a powerful consumer emotion. Loyal retail customers, for example, talk about having a certain comfort level with their favorite store. Loyalties also serve, of course, to reduce risk. Customers talk about going back to companies they trust, that they can rely on, because "I know what I'm getting there!"

REPEAT BUYING IS NOT NECESSARILY LOYALTY

Loyalty is essentially an emotional concept, linked to relationships, and yet many firms seem not to understand or appreciate this. Many businesses continue to define loyalty in behavioral terms. A senior marketing executive of a national retail chain with whom I met recently referred to the fact that their loyal customers appear to be spreading more of their business across a number of competing companies. When I asked how they were defining their loyal customers, I was told that loyalty was captured as a combination of number of visits to their stores and total spend. This narrow view of customer loyalty was compounded by the fact that the data used to measure it were obtained only from customers who use the company's credit card.

There is a great tendency in business to measure or define loyalty entirely in behavioral terms—number of buying trips, frequency of buying, total spend, share of category spend, number of years as a customer, and so on. A recent survey of business leaders conducted by CRMguru asked how they would define customer loyalty. Sixty-four percent define it as repeat buying behavior; 58 percent as customer referrals to friends and colleagues; and 54 percent as a customer's emotional commitment to the relationship.[3]

One of the most frequently referred to models of customer "loyalty" is based on RFM (recency of purchase, frequency of purchase, and monetary value of what is bought). Such an approach to loyalty examines only historic, behavioral measures that are internal to the firm. This type of tool fails to capture the emotional side of loyalty and really addresses behavioral outcomes that may or may not result from loyalty.

Many companies confuse *loyalty* with *retention*—two concepts that are related, but certainly not the same thing. Retention is a behavioral concept. A focus on retention creates a high-risk situation where a company may think customers are a lot more loyal than they really are. Satisfaction with functional aspects of product and service is sufficient to drive retention. It takes emotionally driven loyalty to create solid customer relationships.

Why, then, do some businesses define loyalty primarily if not exclusively in behavioral terms? The answer is often as simple as "That's what we are able to measure most easily." In fact, many companies today capture such information automatically every time a customer interacts with the firm. To obtain a list of our most "loyal" customers, you simply request the information from the customer database. Loyalty defined behaviorally is also a much easier concept to understand, without having to get into all that consumer psychology.

WE'RE IN IT FOR THE POINTS

Frequent-flyer and frequent-shopper programs give the illusion of loyalty. In fact, they are often mislabeled *loyalty* programs. What is it that they are really designed to accomplish? Repeat buying behavior—in other words, retention. The basic premise behind such programs is to *reward* customers for buying more often, for giving the company a greater share of their business. The rewards are extrinsic: points, "free" merchandise or trips. Where true loyalty exists, the rewards are largely intrinsic. One shopper recently observed in an interview that the frequent-shopper "club" of which he is a member feels nothing like any other club to which he has belonged. It never meets and he never associates with other members. Such programs often lock customers in. They create barriers to exit, but they don't on their own lead to true loyalty. Most are in it for the points.

UNDERSTANDING LOYALTY

Of course, customer retention may have little or nothing to do with loyalty. Customers may come back again and again because they perceive no alternative, or they may be locked in to a five-year mortgage or a service contract, or the competition may be perceived to be no better. Or it may simply be a case of customer inertia—they never get around to changing, or they feel switching is just not worth the effort.

A focus on retention is potentially misleading, as a company may be experiencing a very vulnerable form of loyalty. In retail, for example, where customer behavior data are increasingly available, it is useful to examine what motivates and satisfies "loyal" customers. A recent project in which I was involved examined a large sample of such customers, selected from the customer database of a major supermarket chain. We intentionally selected from the database a large sample of customers who were all "loyal"; that is, they were all *behaviorally loyal*. They all bought their groceries at this supermarket just about every week, the company probably accounted for at least 75 percent of their total grocery spend, and they had been shopping there for some time, some of them for many years. Ostensibly, we were dealing with loyal customers. But through a combination of qualitative and quantitative research, we were able to identify some segments of customers whom we described as "functionally loyal" and others who were much more "emotionally loyal."

LOYALTY: FUNCTIONAL OR EMOTIONAL?

The functionally loyal customers appear to be loyal in that their behavior, as reflected in the company's database, is not appreciably different from that of the emotionally loyal. These were customers who visit the company's stores just as frequently and buy roughly the same amount of merchandise.

But when asked why they shop there, it was obvious that their loyalty is driven by the fact that their regular store is conveniently located, it's close to home or they can stop in on their way home from work, it is open 24 hours a day, has wide aisles and lots of checkouts, and "I can get in and out in a hurry."

The customers whom we labeled emotionally loyal, while appearing virtually indistinguishable from the functionally loyal in terms of RFM criteria, indicated that, while the access and convenience factors were important, so too was the fact that they felt comfortable in the stores, were made to feel welcome, were greeted by name, chatted with the "girls at the checkouts," went there with neighbors for coffee, and generally enjoyed the shopping experience. It was in this group that I met the lady who described *her* supermarket as "home away from home." Several observed, "They know me there."

What's intriguing is the fact that both groups demonstrated very similar patterns of shopping behavior—according to an RFM definition of loyalty, both groups were obviously "loyal." The functionally loyal customers, however, reflect a much more vulnerable form of loyalty. They are likely to switch as soon as a competitor offers a more functionally attractive option. They are less likely to seek out a store of that chain if they were to move to another town. The emotionally loyal customer feels an attachment to the firm that transcends functional attributes. This is a loyalty that is likely to last, even in the face of competition that offers a more functionally attractive alternative. Among this group of emotionally loyal customers, we actually interviewed customers who volunteered the fact that they were *proud* to be the firm's customers. They talked about how, over 20 or more years, the firm had made something of itself. Talk about a powerful emotional connection!

WHY SATISFACTION IS LIKE CHOLESTEROL

While the differences between the functionally loyal and the emotionally loyal supermarket shoppers were not obvious in terms of their shopping behavior and purchasing patterns, as we dug more deeply into the customer database we found that, in fact, the emotionally loyal did indeed spend a slightly larger share of their grocery budget at this supermarket and were less likely to buy items on sale. But their comments in the qualitative portion of the project and their scores on the survey questions aimed at measuring the emotional connection clearly demonstrated that they *feel* differently about the firm than do their functionally loyal counterparts.

One of the most interesting findings in the project was that both groups of "loyal" customers scored *exactly the same* on customer satisfaction. Both scored in the 8.1 to 8.2 range. Such a result clearly demonstrates the potentially misleading nature of customer satisfaction scores. While both groups were equally satisfied, one group is clearly more valuable to the company than the other, over the long term.

When we analyzed the survey data more closely, it was obvious that the two groups were equally satisfied with the functional aspects of dealing with the supermarket. The loyalty of the emotionally loyal group, however, was driven by aspects of their interaction with the company that were not important to or not noticed by those whose connection was principally a functional one.

There's a major difference between satisfaction that drives functional loyalty and satisfaction that drives emotional loyalty; hence the notion that, just as there is "good" and "bad" cholesterol, there is good and bad satisfaction. There are simply too many firms and managers who are focused only on customer satisfaction related to product, price, access, convenience, and speed of service—a short-term technical view. Satisfaction is a rational judgment relating to the meeting of expectations about functional aspects of the offer; loyalty and relationships are emotional and driven by surprising and unexpected experiences.

TRANSFORMING THE FUNCTIONALLY LOYAL

A major challenge facing most businesses involves converting occasional customers into regulars and then transforming the functionally loyal into the emotionally loyal. In other words, we have to look for ways to make an emotional connection with customers whose attraction to the company and the rationale for their coming back to buy again has been largely functional.

Is it possible to establish an emotional connection with everyone or to bring all of the functionally loyal over to the emotionally loyal camp? Of course not. There are those whose response is "Get serious; it's a supermarket, for heaven's sake. All I want is to be able to buy groceries; get in and get out." As one banking customer eloquently observed, "I don't want a friend. All I want is a bank."

But is there progress to be made in moving a great many customers closer to the emotionally loyal end of the continuum? Of course there is. And that is very much what this book is about: establishing a strategy that will see you having more emotionally loyal customers a year from now than you have today.

To get there means that we must gain a more complete understanding of customer needs and how we can address them. I'm talking here not about needs in the conventional sense but rather customers' emotional needs—

their need to be appreciated and made welcome, their need to be treated as if they matter, their need *not* to be made to feel frustrated, disappointed, or embarrassed.

FIVE STEPS TO SOLID CUSTOMER RELATIONSHIPS

What drives customer loyalty and relationships? Let's view the components of your value proposition at a series of five levels, each involving progressively more contact with employees and more of a "feelings" dimension to the interaction. As we consider each stage of the *drivers of customer relationships* model, it is useful to think about what it is that your firm offers customers. What is it that you can do at each level that has the potential to produce not only customer satisfaction but ultimately loyalty?

Each successive level in this model involves the satisfaction of progressively higher-order customer needs, and satisfaction of the customer at the lower levels in no way guarantees loyalty at the higher levels. It is quite possible to get things right on the lower levels and create a satisfied customer, but fail to create a loyal customer because of failure to deliver at the higher levels. In this respect, the model borrows conceptually from Abraham Maslow, who is regarded by many to be the father of humanistic psychology.[4] Maslow, writing in the 1950s and 1960s, developed his theory of a "hierarchy of needs," postulating that human beings proceed to satisfy progressively higher levels of needs, beginning with basic physiological needs such as hunger, shelter, and sex, and progressing through safety, social, and self-esteem needs to self-actualization, the stage where an individual achieves inner peace and total satisfaction with his or her life.

As we see in Exhibit 2.1, all companies offer their customers something at each of the five levels of the model. In Chapter 3 we will talk about how each of these five components or levels creates a different form of value for customers. Each level also addresses progressively higher levels of customer needs.

Level 1: The Core

Level 1 is the essence of the offer. It represents the basic product or service that you provide. It's the flight in the case of United Airlines, the clothing on the racks at The Gap, the chicken at KFC, and the checking account at Wells Fargo. This is the most basic of the things being offered to the customer and the one that affords you the least opportunity to differentiate or add value. In a competitive marketplace, you must get the core right; if you don't, the customer relationship will never get started.

Exhibit 2.1   Drivers of Customer Relationships

Stages of Customer Relationship Building	Relationship Drivers
LEVEL 5: The emotional connection: How your firm or brand makes the customer feel	The element of surprise and emotional connection; customer is clearly valued and feels truly appreciated
LEVEL 4: Getting to know us: Interpersonal connection; where the customer meets our people; face-to-face or through technology	The quality and behavior of our people; how they deal with and treat the customer; the interaction or experience
LEVEL 3: Getting it right: Delivering on promises; meeting commitments; accuracy	Delivery is on time; service is prompt; systems, procedures, and processes work as they should
LEVEL 2: Backup support: Systems and processes that enhance and support the core	Access and convenience; technology-based systems and procedures; delivery, scheduling
LEVEL 1: The core: The essence of what the company offers; what it makes or sells, what it does	Functional product and service quality

In many industries, technology and competition have created a situation where the core products and services offered by competing firms are virtually identical. Product quality is so good that it's practically impossible to gain any significant advantage on the basis of the core alone. Customer needs are satisfied at this level to the point where customers look to other components of the offer to add value or to give them a reason to deal with a firm.

At this level you have to get it right. If you don't offer quality at this level, there is little hope of adding value at higher levels—it will be irrelevant. But there is a flip side. Once you do get it right, the customer begins to take it for granted. We see time and time again that the quality of the core product is *not* the main reason why customers choose one company over another.

Level 2: Backup Support

This second level of the drivers of customer relationships includes the support services and systems that enhance the provision of the core: delivery and billing systems, availability and access, hours of service, levels of staffing, communication of information, inventory systems, repair and technical support, help lines and other programs. The main message here is that a customer may become dissatisfied even though the core product is exactly right. A customer may forgo purchasing the car she really wants if delivery will take 10 weeks, or a customer may change Internet service providers because of inadequate help with access problems.

Firms can begin to differentiate themselves and add value by providing support services relating to distribution and information. They can make it easier for customers to deal with them. They can introduce no-hassle returns policies, provide customers with detailed information on the product, or offer 24-hour service. They can arrange to provide routine service on a customer's car while she is out of town so that she won't be inconvenienced by not having it when she needs it. By taking steps to put such systems and policies in place, you begin to add value for the customer and to set your firm apart from the competition.

Level 3: Getting It Right

There is little point in putting in place systems, policies, and procedures unless they are implemented as intended. This third level deals essentially with whether the firm gets the core product and support services right. The emphasis is on doing what the customer was promised. Does Sears deliver the new dishwasher when it said it would? Does the Delta flight arrive at

4:10 P.M., as the schedule indicates it should? Is the room at the Sheraton clean and ready when the guest arrives?

In these examples, there may be nothing wrong with the core product. The company may even have the procedures and systems in place to deliver the core product, but if it doesn't get it right, the processes and systems fail. Customer dissatisfaction and frustration will result from a failure to deliver on customer expectations and your promises.

Up to this level in our model, we are essentially dealing with predictable and functional aspects of the offer: the core product, support systems and processes, and accuracy. These are precisely the things that customers expect from any good company. In fact, as we observed earlier, their conscious, verbalized expectations rarely extend beyond this level. My conclusion, reached over many years, is that if you get things right up to this point, you will have lots of satisfied customers. However, getting things right at the first three levels of the model will get you only to the satisfied stage of your relationship with your customers, not to levels of loyalty or a genuine relationship.

Level 4: Getting to Know Us

This is where you and your employees meet the customer. At Level 4, we deal with the way you interact with customers, either face to face or through technology. Do you make it pleasant and even fun for customers to do business with you? Are your employees courteous, helpful, caring, and are there plenty of them?

Understanding this level indicates that a firm has thought beyond the provision of core product and service, and is focused on the delivery of service at the point where the company meets the customer, regardless of how that interaction takes place. Most of us can recall examples of situations where employees were surly or rude, or simply paid little attention to us, or even ignored us. In such situations, we often walk out and may never go back. This happens even though there was probably nothing wrong with the products or services involved or with the support systems and procedures in place to deliver service quality. One outcome of such an encounter is that the customer feels extremely frustrated because he or she really wanted that jacket or really wanted to eat in that restaurant.

It's at this level where lots of the "little things" happen. For example, in our supermarket research, we found that one of the things that most impressed shoppers is when an employee, when you ask him where to find an item, will get up off the box on which he is sitting while stacking shelves and actually lead you to the item.

Level 5: The Emotional Connection

Finally, let's consider the subtle and not-so-subtle messages that firms often send to customers that may leave them with positive or negative feelings toward the company. Essentially, this addresses the issue of *how we make the customer feel.* Much evidence exists from research that a considerable amount of customer dissatisfaction and defection has nothing to do with the quality of the core product or service or with its price. Indeed, the customer may even be satisfied with most aspects of the interaction with the firm and its employees. But she may leave because of some comment from a staff member or because of some other little thing that goes wrong that may not even be noticed.

Customers often refer to how they are made to feel by companies. I suggest that very few companies that I have encountered pay particular attention to how they and their employees make customers feel. Many interactions leave the customer with negative feelings. Some, probably a smaller number, make the customer feel very good. Many of the events and occasions that elicit these positive and negative feelings are far removed from the provision of the core product or service and may therefore escape the notice of senior managers.

Think about some of the business interactions that you and your friends have had in the past few weeks. I suspect you can recall several that have stuck in your memory and that may even have been the topic of conversation. Think about the things that impressed you or your friends so much that you told others just how pleased you were—the sales clerk who had the out-of-stock shoes sent over from another store across town; the flight attendant who offered her own sweater to your 13-year-old daughter who was feeling cold during the flight.

But perhaps you can recall even more easily situations where you encountered service that fell far short of expectations, when you left without buying or even may have vowed never to go back. Think of how you *felt* on those occasions: disappointed, let down, frustrated, embarrassed. Maybe you felt as strongly as did a woman in Cork, Ireland, who told me and everyone within hearing distance just how she felt about a certain department store and why she will never shop there again!

She had tried to return a pair of jeans that she had bought for her teenage daughter. On the first washing, the dye had run and some of the stitching had come undone. The clerk to whom she spoke called her department manager who, upon examining the jeans, proceeded to lecture the lady in front of other shoppers, telling her that she obviously did not know how to wash jeans. The shopper told me she was "mortified"— probably not the best emotion to be cultivating among our customers.

My point is that all companies, yours included, regularly create emotional reactions from their customers. Where they are positive emotions, they are usually met with higher degrees of loyalty, intentions to go back, and like-lihood of mentioning the positive experience to others. The negative emotions are also talked about, likely more so, and lead to decisions never to return, thereby setting up the high levels of customer churn that plague many companies.

Just as you and your friends and family can easily generate stories, both positive and negative, of experiences you have had with businesses, so too can your customers. Chances are that, right now, some of your customers are sitting around a dinner table or a backyard barbeque telling their friends about an experience they have had with your company and why they will or will not go back. Your challenge is to ensure that the most positive emotional reaction is produced. In the chapters that follow, we'll explore how to do just that.

WHERE DO EXPECTATIONS FIT?

There has been widespread acceptance in recent years of the notion of exceeding customer expectations as a route to achieving customer satisfaction or delight. Many companies blatantly advertise that their goal is to exceed customer expectations—a practice I would advise against, as I will explain later in the book. It is important to understand the role of customer expectations in your customer strategy as customers have expectations related to each of the five stages of the *drivers of customer relationships* model and your objective should be to exceed them, if you are to create an advantage for your firm. As you will see throughout this book, I believe fundamentally in the element of surprise as a strategic tool. You surprise your customers when you exceed their expectations.

At Level 1 in our model, customers expect products to work, that all of the parts will be in the box, and that they will enjoy the use of the product for a reasonable period without failure. They expect the installer to perform the installation properly and the service technician to make the necessary repairs. At Level 2, expectations relate to availability and support: the voice mail system will connect me efficiently and without too much delay; products will be in stock when needed; the technician will have the right tools to do the job; the bills will be accurate. At Level 3, expectations relate to actual performance, to the meeting of promises: the technician will show up on time; the flight will depart on time; the luggage will arrive.

Exhibit 2.2　The Link to Customer Expectations

Stages of Customer Relationship Building	Customer Expectations
LEVEL 5: The emotional connection: How your firm or brand makes the customer feel	Expectations are generally passive; not expecting to be surprised or impressed
LEVEL 4: Getting to know us: Interpersonal connection; where the customer meets our people; face-to-face or through technology	Employees will be helpful, pleasant, courteous, civil, available, knowledgeable
LEVEL 3: Getting it right: Delivering on promises; meeting commitments; accuracy	The firm will meet its commitments; they will generally get things right; accuracy
LEVEL 2: Backup support: Systems and processes that enhance and support the core	Product and service will be conveniently available; firm will have necessary systems and processes in place
LEVEL 1: The core: The essence of what the company offers; what it makes or sells, what it does	The core will work; quality is acceptable; it won't fail

At these first three levels of our model the focus is on delivering against what customers would reasonably expect a firm like ours to do. There may actually be little potential to exceed customer expectations at these levels — there may be little point in the product performing *better* than expected, the technician doesn't need to demonstrate that he brought *more* tools than he needed; the luggage can't show up *early*. But, customers are disappointed, upset and angry when reasonable expectations are not met at these levels. The greatest potential at the first three levels may actually be to create *negative* customer emotions by not meeting expectations.

At Level 4, we begin to see much greater potential to exceed customer expectations and to create genuine emotional value. Customers generally expect employees to be courteous, friendly, knowledgeable and helpful, and it is certainly possible to impress them by employing staff who are *more* friendly and helpful than they will find at the competition. Customers are often heard to make comments like "I really didn't expect them to do that."

Finally at Level 5, the true potential for surprise exists as the firm can exceed expectations that the customer has not even thought of. Here is where we address anticipation and proactivity, taking steps to avert problems and to respond to occasions in ways that will truly surprise and impress, prompting comments to friends like "You will never believe what ____ did for me yesterday."

The link between customer expectations and the establishment of solid relationships is one that we will revisit throughout the book.

WHAT DOES ALL THIS MEAN FOR YOU?

As you consider the various levels of the *drivers of customer relationships* model, keep these key points in mind:

- The things that your firm and your employees do take on progressively more importance in terms of their influence on customer satisfaction and on the creation of relationships with your customers as you move from Level 1 to Level 5.

- As you move from the core product to delivery to interpersonal interaction and on to delivering positive emotions, you are addressing progressively higher-order customer needs; you need to have as broad a view of customer needs as possible.

- Also, as you move from Level 1 of Level 5, you are adding progressively more value for your customers; in fact, you add more valuable forms of value at the higher levels of the model.

- Finally, it is far easier to differentiate your company from the competition by competing at the higher levels of the *drivers of customer relationships* model than at the levels of core and process.

- But you can't simply jump into Levels 4 or 5 without having established solid performance at the lower three levels. Just as you can't produce loyalty without first creating satisfied customers, you can't expect customers to establish an emotional connection with your firm unless you have first established solid product and service quality, and you meet their expectations around delivery and support systems. If you make enough mistakes at the lower levels, you can forget about building relationships.

Endnotes

1. Frederick F. Reichheld, "Loyalty-Based Management," *Harvard Business Review* 71, no. 2 (March–April 1993): 64–73.
2. Susan Fournier, "Consumers and Their Brands: Developing Relationship Theory in Consumer Research," *Journal of Consumer Research* 24 (March 1998): 343–372.
3. Bob Thompson, "The Loyalty Connection: Secrets to Customer Retention and Increase Profits," CRMguru.com, March 2005, p. 2.
4. Abraham H. Maslow, *Maslow on Management* (New York: John Wiley & Sons, 1998).

3

CREATE MEANINGFUL VALUE

Simply put, value lies at the heart of a customer strategy. That's what it's all about: the creation and enhancement of value for your customers. You and your employees must appreciate exactly what components of your *value proposition* are seen by your customers to be creating value for them and which are not. You must have a value creation/addition component of your customer strategy that is compatible with your segmentation and positioning strategies. In other words, you must create and add value that is appropriate for the customers you wish to attract and retain and still be consistent with the kind of company you want to be.

WHAT'S VALUE GOT TO DO WITH IT?

Value perception is a personal thing. Different customers will perceive different things to be valuable. Some look for very personal service, even to be called by their first name, while others would find that too intrusive. Some are focused on low prices, while others are prepared to pay more to get what they want. Some value dealing with firms that make a contribution to the local community, while others feel that is simply not important. Customers will gravitate to and become loyal to those firms and brands that they perceive to be creating value for *them*.

Different firms specialize in the creation of different forms of value— that's what positioning is all about. Therefore, how your competitors create value for their customers should not necessarily influence how you create value for yours. Your value creation strategy should be right for *your* customers and what you want to mean to them.

Why does the title of this chapter refer to "meaningful" value? Simply because some forms of value will mean more to customers than others will.

The challenge to your company is to create the kinds of value that customers will notice and appreciate. If you are creating the same kinds of value as the competition, you will simply be lost in the crowd. The challenge for you is to identify what it is your customers will value and then deliver it. You must create more valuable value. This may not be as easy as it seems.

VALUE CREATION: THE ESSENTIAL ROLE OF THE FIRM

The late Peter Drucker observed that the new definition of the function of business enterprise is *the creation of value and wealth*.[1] The creation of value is the essential responsibility of the firm—value for employees, for customers, for shareholders, and for the communities in which they operate. Creating value for customers has become an essential component of the operation of most companies. But "adding value" is often viewed very simplistically. It has become something of a buzzword, as companies introduce added-value features to their products, or seek to add value for customers by making products easier to use or by bundling telecommunications, cable television, and Internet services together.

All of these may represent value addition for the customer; *but they may not*. It is the customer alone who must determine whether he or she *perceives* value to have been added. If customers do not perceive value, they won't buy. Unless value continues to be perceived and experienced, customers won't be satisfied; and if they are not satisfied, they will drift away to the competition.

Adding value may involve improving the quality of a product by using higher-quality materials or by designing in new features. But adding value may also mean making it easier for customers to do business with you. Braun adds value when it designs new features into its electric shavers. Enterprise Rent-a-Car adds value when it offers to deliver your rental car to your hotel. The server in the dining room at the Ritz-Carlton adds value when she remembers that you like your eggs over easy. You also add value when your employees reduce customer frustration.

When a business attempts to add value for its customers, it must first determine what those customers value. The need for customer insight is critical here—your goal must be to create value that your customers are prepared to pay for and that they will find attractive, not only in a financial sense.

VALUE EQUATION

Value involves a trade-off. Consciously or subconsciously, every time a customer makes a buying decision or decides whether to deal with a particular company, he or she is weighing the pros and cons. It's an equation, with what the customer gets on one side and what he or she has to give on the other.

If the equation looks like this:

$$\text{get} \geq \text{give}$$

the customer will be generally satisfied and will continue to deal with the firm. What the customer gets from the interaction is at least equal to what he or she has to commit. If the "get" is much greater than the "give," then the customer will be well satisfied or even delighted.

But, if the equation looks like this:

$$\text{get} < \text{give}$$

the customer will be dissatisfied and will walk away. If the realization that "get" is less than "give" occurs only after the purchase has been made, the customer is likely not to buy again.

The meaning of give and get goes far beyond the basics of money and core product or service. You might ask yourself what it is that your customers get from dealing with your firm and what you ask of them in return. Chances are, they might get some pretty good products, overnight delivery, a monthly newsletter, and access to some really nice people. In return, they have to give you some money, of course, but they also may have to spend some time placing the order, or navigating your interactive voice response (IVR) telephone system, or waiting in line to be served, or trying to figure out the assembly instructions.

The *costs* that the customer might incur in dealing with a firm include money, time, energy or effort, and various psychological costs. They may also incur certain sensory costs—putting up with noise, drafts, uncomfortable seats, or other negative aspects of the physical setting in which the interaction takes place. The money and time costs are easily measured; however, the energy, sensory, and psychological costs are less evident to the company and are measured subconsciously in the mind of the customer. These are subjective concepts, and customers do not usually calculate these costs consciously. However, from time to time they do make judgmental observations that what they are getting from dealing with the firm is not worth the time or the bother. What they are saying is: "We're not getting value."

IT'S JUST NOT WORTH THE...

When I want to demonstrate to managers the range of factors that customers take into consideration when they subconsciously assess whether they are receiving value, I ask them to think about how customers would complete this sentence: "I'll never go back to that company again. It's just not worth the _____." I use the same technique when interviewing customers in focus groups. When they complete the sentence, they tend to use words like "hassle," "time," "trouble," "bother," "effort," and "grief." It is still surprising to me, and to most managers who are viewing the focus groups, how few customers say "price." This has led me to what I consider a very revealing conclusion—one that some executives find difficult to accept—that, overall, *price is often just not that important in determining the customer's perception of value.*

There are some things that customers are willing to drive across town to buy, or for which they will wait six weeks for delivery, or will willingly pay a higher price. This is their way of dealing with the value equation. Implicitly, they are saying "It's worth it to me to be inconvenienced or to pay more to get the product or service I want." It is through the creation of various forms of value that some firms are able to command higher prices and to avoid being dragged into the quagmire of cutthroat price competition. Established world brands, such as Heinz Ketchup and Chanel No 5, command a price premium and are rarely discounted because they have created such a high level of emotional value for their customers.

WHAT WILL THEY VALUE?

How do we find out if a planned product feature or a service improvement would be considered a valued addition to the range of products and services that the company offers its customers? While there are many research techniques that would allow us to measure the relative attractiveness of proposed improvements, one qualitative technique that I have used for many years actually reveals a great deal about what customers value. First, it is important to recognize that, because value determination involves an implicit equation, value can be created in the customer's mind by adding to one side or reducing the other—by either adding something that is felt to be of value or by reducing or diminishing some aspect of the offer that is viewed to be negative. *Value creation does not always have to involve the addition of something.*

I learn a lot about what customers' value by asking them to describe in detail their dealings with a company or with its products and employees. I ask them to tell me about the interactions, the processes, the detailed steps they go through as they buy the product or avail themselves of the service. I ask them to tell me what could go right and what could go wrong at each step along the way. And I ask them what they like to have happen and what they hope does not happen. I get them to talk about why they would buy this company's product or service rather than a competitor's, and what it would take to move them to another supplier. By asking a series of questions such as these, I can build up an understanding of the interaction between the customer and the company and of which aspects or elements of that interaction are satisfying and which are potentially dissatisfying. It is then a rather short step to conclude that we can create value by doing more of the things that the customer finds attractive and fewer of those that are potential dissatisfiers.

WHAT IS VALUE?

What would your customers value if you would or could do it? You create value for your customers insofar as you address their needs. If you can better address those needs, they will choose your firm or brand. If you can do better than they were expecting, you'll create surprise and delight, and they will not only come back but will be prepared to pay more for the privilege and they'll tell their friends.

Value is a very personal thing, bound up in the perceptions of the individual consumer. As discussed earlier, what represents value for one customer will not necessarily represent value for another. Just as customers look for different things when they buy, they will attach greater or lesser value to many of the components of the value package, and will do so in different situations. What customers' value is very much related to the *context* in which they find themselves at a particular time. For example, what we consider to be of value when we are traveling on a business trip to London or Chicago will not be the same things that are valued when we travel with the family on a holiday to Disney World.

We need to consider a very holistic view of how consumers view value, at least in a subconscious sense. My experience would suggest that, if you simply ask customers to comment on the value they are receiving in a certain situation, they will usually answer in monetary terms; but if you probe beneath the surface, they actually place considerable value on things that have nothing to do with the price they are paying. So customer value is not simply value for money; it's much more complex than that.

Morris Holbrook, in an insightful analysis of customer value, observed that value is "a relativistic (comparative, personal, situational) preference characterizing a subject's experience of interacting with some object."[2] One very important point that Holbrook makes is that value is associated with an experience in that it pertains not only to the acquisition of an object but to the consumption and use of its services. This is an especially useful view of what value entails when defined by the customer. It is not at all limiting and does not focus on price or on tangible objects. Rather it gives value the scope it deserves and the scope that customers intend. Customers do define value very broadly, even though they may not use the terminology. They know, in very broad terms, what they get in dealing with a firm, and they know roughly what it "costs" them to get it and whether it is "worth it."

CUSTOMER'S VIEW OF VALUE

Value perception is a predictor of customer behavior and loyalty. Buyers who are considering a purchase will scan their options and develop a small set of brands to consider. The customer will purchase the product or service that he or she perceives to deliver the most value. This assessment of value in the products or services being considered, and the postpurchase evaluation of value received, may take place at a very subjective or even subconscious level. The customer will likely not weigh each element of the product or service offer and do a mental calculation of which offers the best value or whether value has been received. He or she may not even use the term *value* but may simply decide to buy one product or another. There is, however, an implicit assessment of value being made whenever a customer faces the inevitable choice involved in a purchase situation or a decision whether to stay or leave. It will be a judgment call—very appropriate terminology for a situation that is highly judgmental. The customer weighs anticipated benefits against current and anticipated costs. The conclusion may be: "I didn't get good value there. I won't be back" or simply "It's not worth it to me."

The customer must decide whether value is being created or added, and customers define value in many different ways—some see value in the lowest price. But current research would have us conclude that maybe as few as 20 percent of customers in any given product or service category are truly price driven—that is, they regularly look for the lowest prices available. This leaves 80 percent or more who define value more broadly and who care about more than price alone. While this percentage is certainly a rough estimate, and although the measurement of something as ephemeral as price sensitivity is subjective and prone to variability across product categories and situations, the principle is nevertheless an important one: *Some large percentage of customers are indeed not particularly focused on price.* They want value and they define it on their own terms. In fact, I regularly meet customers who tell me that they would willingly pay *more* if the company would only perform or behave in a certain way.

VALUE HIERARCHY

Your company can create added value for your customers in many different ways. In the *drivers of customer relationships* model introduced in Chapter 2, we see that different forms of value should be created at each stage in the evolution of the relationship and that what is suitable to deliver and enhance the core at Level 1 is not the same kind of value that will sustain an emotional connection with the customer at Level 5. Therefore, it's useful to think about a *progression of value creation* that demands a higher level of value creation as we move toward a focus on customer relationships.

As we see in Exhibit 3.1, the kind of value needed at Level 1, where the emphasis is on the core product or service and on delivering value for money, is not especially complex and is related principally to product development and improvement. To create value at Level 2, we need to develop and implement various support systems to ensure access and convenience, and at Level 3 we strive for reliability and the delivery of technically correct service. A more individualized kind of value is added at Level 4, where service is personal and customized to the customer. Finally, the highest-order value in the value hierarchy is added at Level 5, where the firm addresses the emotional needs of its customers.

Progressively higher-order value is added for customers as a company moves through the various stages of developing its customer strategy, from the offering of a basic core product or service, to the enhancement of service quality, to promising or even guaranteeing its products and service, to personalization and on to the establishment of an emotional connection.

Value creation is an integral component of the customer strategy, and the firm must realize that different approaches of value creation will represent different levels of perceived value to the customer, that some forms of value are, in fact, more valuable than others.

VALUE PROPOSITION:
FUNCTIONAL AND EMOTIONAL COMPONENTS

The concept of the *value proposition* is a useful one; your firm must have its own value proposition. It focuses attention on what you can offer customers that will be valued and that will, as a result, contribute to the progression toward relationship building. But, as with many words that creep into the language of business, the term *value proposition* is often used rather loosely to refer to many different aspects of what the company is offering the customer. Consistent with our earlier discussion of value, companies must

Exhibit 3.1 Progression of Value Creation

Stages of Customer Relationship Building	Value Created
LEVEL 5: The emotional connection: How your firm or brand makes the customer feel	Higher-order value; customer is impressed and grateful; feels unique; problems are solved, needs addressed
LEVEL 4: Getting to know us: Interpersonal connection; where the customer meets your people; face-to-face or through technology	More personal forms of value, individualized, respect; employees are caring and empathetic
LEVEL 3: Getting it right: Delivering on promises; meeting commitments; accuracy	Reliability; be there when needed; errors are minimized; superior technical service
LEVEL 2: Backup support: Systems and processes that enhance and support the core	Access and convenience; make it easy to deal with us; choice and selection
LEVEL 1: The core: The essence of what the company offers; what it makes or sells, what it does	Product quality; value for money; good product for the price charged

have a holistic view of their value proposition. It is literally everything that the company offers or is capable of doing for its customers. It is both the "harder" functional side and the "softer" emotional side of what the customer receives from the company.

Many executives seem to think that the only way to create value for the customer is through modifications to or improvements in the core product or how it is delivered, or through manipulation of the price. Such is, of course, not the case. But it is indicative of the fact that some managers are often focused on the hard, functional side of the value proposition because that's usually the basis on which they are rewarded. As discussed in Chapter 2, performing the functional aspects of the value proposition well, while necessary, will only allow you to achieve relatively high levels of customer satisfaction. If it's loyalty you are after, then you must focus on the emotional aspects. I am convinced that, while managers tend to gravitate toward the harder, more tangible or functional side, customers pay more attention to the softer, emotional elements when deciding whether to continue to buy a brand or deal with a company.

Let me illustrate with the example of a food distribution company with which I was working a few years ago. In my first meeting with the management team, I asked them how they evaluated their company performance in dealing with their customers. They proudly pointed to their commitment to the concept of the "perfect order." This very sophisticated company operated some of the most impressive automated warehouses I have ever seen. Their computerized inventory management, materials handling, and logistics systems were equally impressive and led to very detailed reports being produced that measured performance of the company's divisions against the "perfect order" standard.

That standard involved striving for excellence in delivery and distribution; everything the company did was bar coded, scanned, timed, and measured in the interest of achieving perfect delivery of the customer's order—on time, 100 percent fulfillment, no backorders, no stockouts, no damaged goods. Isn't that what customers want? The answer is "Yes, but . . ."

The management team's commitment to the perfect order, while admirable, addresses only half of the picture. Let me illustrate. When two-hour in-depth interviews were conducted with some of the company's clients, we found that the perfect order was, to a very great extent, expected; isn't that what a good food distributor should do? It was not seen to be a differentiator. When, near the end of my interview with the food service director of a seniors' home, I asked what was the most troublesome aspect of her job, what literally keeps her awake at night, she didn't mention on-time delivery, or yield management, or staffing the kitchen—any of the predictable things that one would typically associate with her role. She said that her most difficult challenge was "making dinner interesting" for her elderly residents.

Another food service manager, when asked her what my client might do to improve service to her company, suggested that when making the delivery, the driver should pick up the stray pieces of cardboard that occasionally blow off the back of the truck and across the parking lot.

What we see in both of these cases, and there were numerous other examples, as there are in virtually all projects of this type, is the customers' focus on softer elements of the value proposition and a certain taken-for-granted attitude toward what management thinks are the most important components of the value proposition. While management is often focused almost solely on the creation of functional value, their customers, in my experience, usually judge performance on how well the company is performing on the softer side.

GIVING AND TAKING AWAY

Going back to our earlier observation that value creation involves an equation, by definition, we can add value by adding to one side of the value equation or proposition or by taking away from the other, as illustrated in Exhibit 3.2. Also, as suggested in Chapter 2, using the *drivers of customer relationships* model, a company is able to add progressively more value for the customer as it moves from focusing on the core product or service offering, to focusing more on service delivery and accuracy and on the interpersonal contact between customers and the company. Ultimately the greatest value—emotional value—is added when the company is able to create an environment where there is a genuine, strong emotional connection between the company and its customers: in other words, a genuine relationship.

To illustrate how your company can get beyond the basic levels of customer satisfaction and add value to your offer to the customer, let's return to the *drivers of customer relationships* model and consider the five levels and what you can add or eliminate at each level.

Level 1: The Core

This is the basic element of your firm's value proposition. If you get it wrong at this level, you can forget about adding value higher up, because the customer simply won't care. There is often little in the core product or service that distinguishes one company's offering from another's. Of course, you can

Exhibit 3.2 Value Creation and the Drivers of Customer Relationships

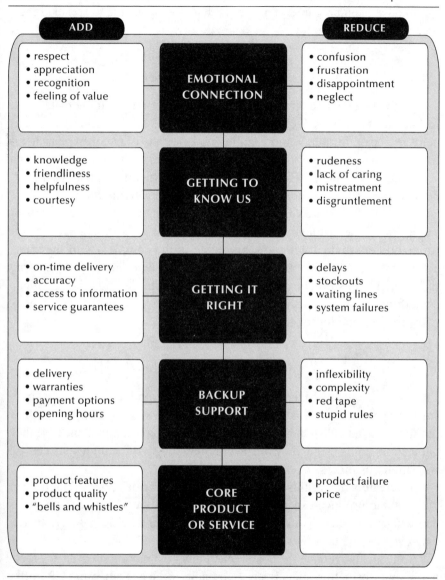

ADD		REDUCE
• respect • appreciation • recognition • feeling of value	**EMOTIONAL CONNECTION**	• confusion • frustration • disappointment • neglect
• knowledge • friendliness • helpfulness • courtesy	**GETTING TO KNOW US**	• rudeness • lack of caring • mistreatment • disgruntlement
• on-time delivery • accuracy • access to information • service guarantees	**GETTING IT RIGHT**	• delays • stockouts • waiting lines • system failures
• delivery • warranties • payment options • opening hours	**BACKUP SUPPORT**	• inflexibility • complexity • red tape • stupid rules
• product features • product quality • "bells and whistles"	**CORE PRODUCT OR SERVICE**	• product failure • price

add new product features and improve quality, but gaining any permanent competitive advantage at this level is very difficult, especially when your competitors are delivering pretty good or even identical core products.

You can reduce product failure or you can simply drop your price, but this is often a futile exercise. This typically attracts the price-conscious customer, builds no customer loyalty, and results in your leaving money on the table by missing opportunities to attract less price-motivated customers who would have been prepared to pay more, had you been able to create higher-order value in their minds.

Level 2: Backup Support

This is the level where firms add services that are intended to create value for the customer by reducing nonmonetary costs. Adding services such as delivery, repair, installation, warranties, and a variety of payment plans helps to differentiate your company and provides added value. It's mainly about access and convenience. But while such services can differentiate your business or brand, they too are easily replicated by the competition.

You can also create value at this level by taking away those elements of service that your customers find frustrating. This is where you make it easier for customers to deal with you, by reducing the complexity of the interaction, by being more flexible, by reducing "red tape," and by eliminating the rules that customers feel are absolutely stupid. Doing this may mean something as obvious as making it possible for your customers to speak with real live employees when they want to.

Level 3: Getting It Right

This is the stage at which many companies are proud to excel: They strive for the "perfect order" and impeccable logistics. They deliver on their promises and establish themselves as leaders in "service excellence." If they get it right at this stage, they mistakenly feel they will be highly successful with their customers.

To create value at this level, you provide superior service. You deliver on time and produce exactly what was promised. Service is completed as and when you said it would be. You do whatever it takes to get it right. You may even decide to offer service guarantees.

You can also reduce the cost to customers by making it easier for them to obtain information and advice. Companies such as FedEx and UPS offer online tracking of shipments so that customers know precisely when their packages will be delivered. This reduces the anxiety, time, and money associated with owning and using the service, thereby increasing value for the customer. Value can be created at this level through the reduction or elimination of delays, stockouts, errors in order filling, systems failures, and employee mistakes. Anything that you can do to reduce such errors will enhance service delivery and reliability.

Up to this point in our value creation process, it is important to realize that we are creating largely *functional* value that drives customer satisfaction. With customer expectations increasing, more and more customers are expecting companies to get things right and to perform well at the lower three levels of our model. A client of mine observed that, up to this point, we are dealing with table stakes; if you can't get these things right, how can you expect to gain an advantage over the competition?

Level 4: Getting to Know Us

It's at this fourth level that you have an opportunity to personalize the interaction with customers, regardless of whether that interaction takes place with your employees or through technology-based channels including the Internet. Customers often decide whether to continue to deal with a firm based on how they are handled by members of staff or how easy it is to deal with the company. Employees who are friendly, helpful, understanding, personable, courteous, and empathetic are, for obvious reasons, preferred.

The solution to creating value at this level, therefore, is found in decisions relating to the hiring and training of your people and to the design of customer contact technologies, including your Web site. You are setting out to create friendliness, helpfulness, courtesy, and ease of operation. But you are also focused on creating value by reducing or eliminating situations in which the customer encounters rudeness, a lack of caring, and too few employees to serve him. Many budding customer relationships are ended, despite excellence at the lower levels of our model, because of an upsetting encounter with an uncaring employee or a frustrating Web site or IVR system.

Level 5: Emotional Connection

How you make your customers feel is the fifth driver of customer relationships and the highest level at which to add emotional value. Creating value at this level requires discipline and a focus on how the customer is likely to feel about dealing with your company. Many firms are simply not very good at this, possibly because it requires a different way of looking at the customer. Product quality, fair prices, and on-time delivery are important (even necessary), but if your driver doesn't pick up the cardboard that blows off his truck, the value provided is diminished. By the way, how do you think that customer was feeling as she watched the cardboard boxes blow across the parking lot?

Creating value at this highest level is simple—or at least the concept is simple: Look for ways to create positive emotional reactions from your customers and to reduce or eliminate negative emotions. You and your employees must be constantly thinking past the obvious things, to ask yourselves how your behavior, systems, performance, rules, and reactions might make the customer feel.

Customer feelings and emotions are often deeply held and will have a profound influence on whether a customer will continue to do business with you in the future. But where do these emotions come from? They arise at each of the four previous levels. You can make a customer feel very frustrated by making it difficult for her to assemble a piece of garden furniture or by failing to include the wrench needed to attach the bolts to the frame—both product problems. You create a sense of undervaluing your loyal customers by offering lower prices to switchers to return. You create a sense of not being appreciated or wanted when customer phone calls and e-mail message are not returned.

This view of value creation in the context of the *drivers of customer relationships* model serves to illustrate a number of very important points:

- Value can be added or diminished at each of the five levels of the model as you strive to satisfy progressively higher-order needs for the customer.

- You can create functional value successfully at the lower levels of the model only to see it destroyed at a higher level. Simply put, you can have the best product and fail to deliver it on time and make the customer very disappointed.

- The most important value is emotional value, which is most likely to be created at the top two levels. Although we place emotions at the top of the model, we realize that emotions, both positive and negative, can also be generated at each of the lower levels.

- Functional forms of value are easier for managers to conceptualize and deliver but will only get you to satisfaction, not to a relationship.

- The key to moving beyond satisfaction to a relationship is to offer more and better value; emotional value is better value because it's longer-lasting and less easily copied.

- Functional value can be created for most customers in a similar way (price, convenience, etc.)—that is, the same value is delivered to all—while emotional value is personal and must be tailored to the individual.

CREATING MORE VALUABLE VALUE

Let's turn our attention now to the differences between functional and emotional value creation and why one is more likely to gain you a competitive edge.

There are many ways to create functional value, most of which are entirely predictable and what one would expect of a company that is trying to serve its customers well. Functional value creation is essentially what your customers will suggest you do better if you were to ask them. Unfortunately, it also happens to be the most easily copied and the least likely to result in the creation of meaningful, long-lasting value for the customer.

The creation of functional value is not especially creative or strategic. It's linear thinking: How can we do better what we already do? It's about creating more value for money, better quality, lower prices, longer opening hours, greater variety, technical service improvements, and better information. Increasingly, customers expect companies to do well on the functional side. When you rise to the occasion, you will have more satisfied customers.

But to build customer loyalty and genuine relationships, you must add emotional value. We call it emotional value because it provokes an emotional response in your customers. The question is how to do it. Essentially, you have to be constantly thinking of how you can be more relevant to your customers, how you can play a greater role in their lives, make a connection with them, strike a chord, speak their language, resonate with them, make it possible for them to accomplish things, associate with things that are important in their lives, create positive experiences.

MEANINGFUL VALUE CREATION: BEING LATERAL

To create emotional value, you must think outside that box inside which most of us operate every day. In most of my dealings with business executives, I find that, while most accept without question the need to create value for their customers, they have a rather limited view of how to actually do it. Consequently, most companies' value-add strategies involve an emphasis on new product innovation, product improvements, and advances in service delivery. In other words, they look to improve the things that are already components of the value proposition. When faced with a competitive challenge, the tendency is to strive to do better what they already do. Many companies do not demonstrate a lot of evidence on initiatives that result in the company doing *different* things.

Many companies have clearly bought in to the notion that success lies in exceeding customer expectations. In fact, some even go so far as to promise to do so in their advertising—thereby drawing attention to their goals and setting themselves up for failure. Phil Knight and Nike had it right: Don't tell them you are going to do it, *just do it.*

But what exactly do companies mean when they set out to exceed customer expectations? In most cases, they are attempting to exceed those expectations that customers typically associate with the situation at hand—to exceed expectations relating to the things that customers typically will expect us to do in this situation. This involves a *linear* exceeding of expectations—doing better, faster, more accurately, those things that we are expected to do.

The greater value for both customers and your firm comes from the *lateral* exceeding of expectations—doing things that they simply were not expecting you to do; surprising them in a positive way. This is where emotional value is created. Whenever you can elicit a response like "You didn't have to do that" or "I wasn't expecting you to offer me that," you know you have made a good impression.

The lateral exceeding of expectations involves adding something new to the value proposition. When auto dealerships first began to wash customers' cars when they were in for service, this represented a departure from what typically happened—a departure from the context. Such behavior constituted a small "Wow!" for many customers who were pleasantly surprised when they picked up a clean car. Now, when most dealers routinely wash customers' cars, what was once surprising has become commonplace, an entrenched part of the value proposition. Auto dealers have to look for other ways to conduct themselves differently that customers will find valuable.

Some retailers have succeeded in establishing an emotional connection with the customer by developing a different business model, a different way of behaving. The result is surprising. Customers tell me that they "love" to shop at T.J. Maxx in the United States and at Winners in Canada because they never know what they will find. These retailers epitomize and capitalize on the view of shopping as hunting. Women discuss enthusiastically the fact that they have to go to these stores every week so that they won't miss a great "find." They enthuse about the thrill of the hunt and share their successes with anyone who will listen.

A possibly surprising example of emotional bonding has emerged in recent years, as women increasingly talk of their enjoyment of shopping at The Home Depot. What is it that causes such an obvious attachment to a building supplies store? This company has responded strategically to the phenomenon of home design and decor as front and center topics in the media. Its merchandising has changed so as to embrace the phenomenal increase in interest. But possibly more important is the repositioning of The Home Depot as not simply a place to buy things but as your partner in making your home more attractive: "You can do it; we can help." This is reinforced through The Home Depot's behavior, offering seminars and workshops to teach you how to lay ceramic tile or to build that tree house.

These companies create emotional value by doing different things, not by doing things that are typically expected of companies in their categories. Smaller firms can easily create surprises for their customers by stepping outside the box to deliver something different: the video rental store that sets aside the new release for a customer simply because they know she will enjoy it; the hotel bellman who offers to have the guest's brochures and presentation materials sent to his office by courier so he doesn't have to pack them in his already-heavy suitcase; the auto dealer that offers to have the customer's serviced car ready for him at the airport when he returns from the business trip.

The T.J. Maxx and The Home Depot examples illustrate how some firms have entrenched a different way of conducting themselves into their business model—they have decided to do things differently, to stop behaving predictably—but we already see other companies in their categories emulating them.

The video store and car dealer examples illustrate occasional surprises, situations that individual employees have seized on to address a customer's problem or to make a positive impression. They are examples of what I call "planned spontaneity." Those companies that have succeeded in driving home to their employees the importance of seizing opportunities to impress are well on their way to creating emotional value and to establishing a connection with their customers. They make things possible, they address unvoiced needs, they do things customers would not expect us to do.

THINK CUSTOMER CONTEXT: WHAT ARE THEY GOING THROUGH?

To create emotional value, firms must first understand and appreciate the *context* in which customers are operating. They are buying this product or service in order to accomplish something. They want to succeed at something or to look good in someone's eyes. Everything we sell makes something possible. We need to know what that something is. To dig more deeply into customer context, we need greater insight, a topic to which we will turn our attention in Chapter 8.

To deliver emotional value to your customers, you and your employees will need to think beyond the obvious, to be constantly asking "What else could we help them with?" or "What else could we do that will make a last-ing impression on them?" Think about what customers are facing as they go about buying your product or service. How can you and your firm play a greater role as a partner in helping customers achieve their objective?

It is useful to think about the customer context at four levels, as illus-trated in Exhibit 3.3. In most high-involvement or complex purchase situ-ations, there are (1) things that customers must do; (2) things they realize must be done and plan to get around to; (3) things that they will encounter and hadn't even thought of; and (4) things that they are not likely to think of. The more your firm can anticipate customer needs at Levels 3 and 4, the more you can surprise and delight them. Consider the example of a family hiring a moving company to move their belongings to a new home in a different city.

Context is important here because the family expects the moving com-pany to do well what is expected of a moving company—the safe and timely moving of their belongings from one city to the other with little or no break-age. This is the shared context and shared expectations of both company and customer. It is unlikely that the family has any greater expectations of the moving company beyond its performing these services in a friendly, helpful,

Exhibit 3.3   The Customer Context: Identifying Where to Add Value

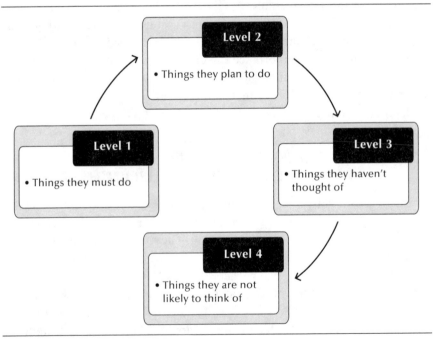

and efficient manner. At the same time, it is likely that the moving company is mainly focused on moving the family's possessions safely and delivering them on time. Attempts at adding value to this core service might extend to placing mats on hardwood floors, wrapping especially valuable pieces in extra padding, and ensuring that employees are pleasant and easy to deal with. In other words, attempts to add value are predictable, directly related to the core service, and intended to increase levels of customer satisfaction.

But the customers in our home-moving example are operating within a context that extends well beyond moving things from one location to another. This is only one service needed within the much bigger challenge of moving a family to a new home. Many other elements of the moving experience represent situations where the family may need assistance or information. These may be viewed as extensions of the customer context and are opportunities for the moving firm to extend its value proposition into areas that would lead to customer delight. To add emotional value for customers, managers need contextual insight that will allow them to better understand what customers are experiencing at several levels.

If it were inclined to act outside the conventional moving company box and address the needs of its customers at these levels, a firm might offer advice and information that the family would consider valuable. Most new home buyers will have addressed the kinds of activities implicit at Level 1—arranging for financing; electrical, telephone, Internet, and cable TV hookup; unpacking of boxes—simply because they would have to do so in order to move into their new home.

But a moving company might provide at Level 2 a list of local companies that will do minor renovations or that offer pool cleaning and lawn maintenance services. It might provide information on garbage and recycling services, help the family to notify friends and businesses of their change of address—all things the family will have to do at the time of moving.

At Level 3, the moving firm might surprise or delight the family by dealing with things that they will need on moving day or shortly thereafter. The firm might provide a list of approved child care facilities and trained babysitters, nearby medical clinics, and supermarkets. By offering vouchers for dinner at a nearby restaurant to help them cope with the chaos associated with moving day, it sends the message "We know what you are going through and want to help you out."

Finally, operating at Level 4, an observant moving company would have noted that the family has two children ages 9 and 12, an aging golden Labrador, and a 2004 Honda Accord, and could provide information to the family on neighborhood veterinary clinics, licensed music teachers and dance studios, minor league soccer programs, and the name and telephone number of the service manager at the local Honda dealership—information that the family may find very useful in the weeks after moving in, but would not have gotten around to finding for themselves.

By attempting to understand and appreciate the context in which its customers are operating, the company opens itself up considerably, and its employees will think of other things they might be doing to help the family make the transition to a new home. Doing this will cultivate emotional value and cement a relationship, driving word-of-mouth and referral business.

VALUE: THE ESSENCE OF THE CUSTOMER STRATEGY

Managers must realize that, unless value is created and regularly added for their customers, they will not have succeeded in creating any reason for the customer to stay. Without value being provided regularly, customers will perceive no differential advantage of one company over another; thus no competitive advantage is created. Without value being created, there is no customer satisfaction, because customers do not willingly continue to do business with companies that provide them with little of value. And without sustained customer satisfaction, relationships do not develop.

Thus, understanding and appreciating the creation of value for customers are critical components in a company's customer strategy. Value may be created for customers in many different ways, some much more valuable than others. To achieve a relationship with customers, you must create emotional value. You must move past the provision of predictable product and service quality and great value for money to do things that strike a chord with customers and sends a message that you have noticed something that others have not. You create emotional value when you help customers out, associate with the things that are central to their lives, show that you are a member of their community, remind them of pleasant experiences, and make them feel special.

In Chapter 4 we will examine in more depth the building blocks of the emotional connection with customers—the kinds of emotions that you will want to create and those to avoid at all costs.

Endnotes

1. Peter F. Drucker, "The Next Information Revolution," *Forbes,* August 24, 1998.
2. Morris B. Holbrook, "The Nature of Customer Value: An Axiology of Services in the Consumption Experience," in *Service Quality: New Directions in Theory and Practice,* ed. Roland T. Rust and Richard L. Oliver (Thousand Oaks, CA: Sage Publications, 1994), p. 27.

4

YOU MEAN A LOT TO THEM

Suddenly, all companies are trying to demonstrate that they are customer centric, or customer focused, or customer driven. Where has this enthusiasm for the customer come from? And isn't it just a bit ironic to suggest that marketing departments, in particular, should now begin to focus on customers, thereby implying that they haven't been that inclined in the past? I always thought that marketing was all about serving the customer.

I was a little intrigued, therefore, to learn recently that Best Buy, the giant electronics retailer, had been experimenting with offering its customers something different: *service*. Some analysts seemed surprised that sales growth in the first quarter of 2005 was twice as high in the company's new "customer centricity" stores as in those that continued to sell the old way, without personal service delivered by knowledgeable staff.[1]

BECOMING CUSTOMER CENTRIC

Today most companies are focusing on building customer loyalty rather than simply trying to sell more stuff. The concept of "relationship marketing" began to creep onto the pages of marketing publications during the 1980s, led largely by the work of Leonard Berry of Texas A&M University who made mention of the concept in an American Marketing Association presentation in 1983.[2] This new view of marketing also reflected a change of emphasis within the field that suggested that it's just as important—or possibly even more important—to focus on keeping customers as it is to emphasize getting them through the door in the first place.

The relatively new interest in customer retention (and eventually relationships) is almost directly attributable to the availability of customer data made possible by advanced information systems. In many firms, it became possible within the past 20 years to demonstrate the flow of revenue that is attributable to a customer returning repeatedly. As data became increasingly available, information technology (IT) systems revealed what many knew intuitively to be true: that customers became considerably more valuable the longer they stayed.

During the 1990s, more and more companies jumped on the customer relationship bandwagon, and the IT industry started paying attention to the information that firms would need to support their relationship-building initiatives. Bob Thompson, president and CEO of CRMguru.com, indicates that by the mid-1990s, a number of competing terms were being applied to IT-enabled relationship marketing, including TERM (technology enabled relationship marketing), but by the late1990s, CRM (customer relationship management) had emerged as the industry-standard terminology.

As the emphasis on the building of customer relationships became more mainstream, as the acronym CRM began to appear more regularly in the vocabulary of senior executives, and as more companies began to label themselves "customer-centric," I became progressively more disillusioned with the concept as it was being discussed and applied in many organizations. My concerns centered on the use of the word *relationship*. I had a clear view in my mind of how most people would use the term and the context in which they would think that they have a relationship with someone or with an organization. My view was and still is that the word *relationship* is one that has special meaning for most people and is reserved for those situations where there is a genuine feeling and an emotional connection between—in most cases—two people. I feel very strongly that, if we are going to start referring to our ongoing interactions with customers as "relationships," then we had better understand what customers mean by the term.

NATURE OF CUSTOMER RELATIONSHIPS

It is essential, then, that we consider relationships from the customer's perspective. Companies often delude themselves into thinking that they have a relationship with customers if those customers buy their products and services regularly. But customers understand the difference between repeat buying, which is often based on convenience, price, or other nonemotive factors, and situations where they go back to the same companies and brands again and again because they feel some special connection with them. In that sense, customers often feel the same kind of emotional attachment toward certain companies and brands as they do toward friends, family members, and colleagues.

I know, some of you are saying right now: "Hold on a minute, I could never have the same feelings about a product or company as I have toward my spouse or kids." I agree. But as customers, we often express the same *kinds* of emotions toward businesses as we express toward people to whom we are close. Some firms and brands play an important role in our lives. We miss them when they are not around. And occasionally we are frustrated by them.

Work done by consumer psychologists on the attachment that humans develop toward certain personal objects and possessions, and on the association of meaning with such objects, offers a great deal of information about customer relationships with companies and brands.[3] Certain things that we own and associate with special events or that were handed down from parents or grandparents occupy a special place in our lives. We would be devastated if they were lost, stolen, or destroyed. Often we associate that same feeling with companies and brands. We feel a loss when a business with which we have been dealing for years closes its doors. We are disappointed or even angry when a brand is no longer available or when a trusted brand changes its formulation. We feel let down when a company, on which we thought we could rely, fails to deliver on time.

Some firms or brands become special to us. They occupy a special place in our lives. We adopt a possessive way of referring to them: "my hairdresser," "my dry cleaner," "my local pub." We develop a high degree of comfort with them; we trust them, we rely on them; and we may even get to the stage where we feel we can't live without them.

THEY KNOW THEM WHEN THEY FEEL THEM

My view of what constitutes a relationship was buoyed by the feedback I received from customers when I asked them in client research to describe companies with which they enjoy dealing and those to which they would go back time and time again, where they feel comfortable. Most people have no difficulty bringing such companies to mind.

However, customers also can name companies with which they refuse to deal or those where the relationship is strained. In discussion, it is obvious that their disappointment often has little to do with products and services or with the prices being charged and a great deal more to do with the interaction with the company and its employees and with how customers feel about how they are treated.

WHAT IS A RELATIONSHIP ANYWAY?

One of the drawbacks inherent in much of what has been written on CRM is the lack of consideration given to what actually constitutes a relationship.

We are, for the most part, missing a clear view of when a customer relationship actually exists. It is conceivable that a certain connection with a firm may be termed a relationship by some customers, while others may perceive the same contact to be merely an interaction, devoid of the elements or characteristics that, in their minds, would constitute a relationship. Given that there is a personal and arbitrary distinction between an interaction and a relationship, it may be useful to examine what I believe to be the essential building blocks of customer relationships.

The customer, as the object of the firm's attention, must be first and foremost in any discussion of customer relationships. *The objective must be to build a positive relationship from the perspective of the customer, not of the firm.* If given a choice, customers simply won't return to a firm toward which they feel negative emotions. It is, therefore, possible that firms may feel that they have a relationship with their customers, when no such relationship exists in the customers' minds. These companies do not understand that a relationship with a customer requires that it be a two-way interaction. There has to be a desire on the part of both parties to want to develop a relationship; more important, the desire to maintain the relationship must be grounded in emotions and feelings.

THERE'S NO EMOTION

There is something fundamental missing in what is currently referred to as CRM: the emotional component of the relationship. Many CRM initiatives pay no attention to how the customer is *made to feel.* Once you get past the buzzwords and start to assess what companies are trying to accomplish, you realize that many really have no concept of what it means to have a relationship with their customers, and they have no strategy in place that will lead them to genuine relationships.

A relationship is, especially from the perspective of customers, an emotional concept. If their dealings with a firm are characterized by purely functional contact, then they are unlikely to develop any strong feelings toward that firm. The objective of a customer strategy, therefore, must be to establish a positive emotional connection between the company and its customers. To get there, it helps to understand what role emotions play in the establishment of relationships.

Emotions arise in response to a conscious or subconscious appraisal by customers of their dealings with a firm or brand. They are developed over time, based on the ongoing exposure to and experience with the company. If customer expectations are regularly exceeded and positive experiences characterize the interaction, then over time the customer's appraisal will be a positive one and a positive emotional connection will develop with the firm or brand.

Emotions are also quite different from customer satisfaction, in that they are future oriented and imply action that is to be taken by the customer. Satisfaction is a short-term judgment call on the part of the customer: Did they or did they not do what they said they would? A customer's feelings toward a company, however, predict future behavior toward that firm. Customers' emotional responses to how they have been treated may be either positive or negative. If negative emotions, such as frustration, confusion, anger, or embarrassment, are elicited, chances are the customer will look for other options. Conversely, customers return again and again to companies that make them feel comfortable, appreciated, relieved, and even proud.

If you are serious about building solid relationships with your customers, then an essential component of your customer strategy must be the continuous eliciting of positive emotions and the building of an emotional connection with customers.

HIERARCHY OF EMOTIONS

A variety and range of emotional responses may be elicited through your interaction with your customers. Some of those emotions are more intense or strongly felt than others, and it is the most intense positive emotions that have the greatest potential to contribute to the formation of solid relationships. The degree to which an emotional response is elicited through your interaction with your customers and the intensity of that response will depend on a number of factors:

- As discussed in Chapter 3, the circumstances or context in which the customer is operating will contribute to the intensity of the response.
- The salience or importance of the situation, what the customer wishes to accomplish and her degree of involvement.
- The customer's expectations based on previous experience with the firm and on the reputation as communicated through advertising and other forms of communication.
- The atmosphere or ambiance in which the interaction takes place.

Thus, a customer is likely to feel more intense positive or negative emotions when negotiating the purchase of an expensive item or an emotionally charged one, such as a wedding gown, than she is when making a more routine purchase. Where the customer is relaxed and feels little pressure, something going wrong may represent an irritant that is unlikely to elicit a strong negative emotional reaction. That same thing going wrong in a high-pressure setting may elicit much greater intensity of response.

In English and other languages, literally hundreds of words have an emotional meaning or connection. So many words are needed to describe emotions simply because emotions are both subtle and personal; we need to be able to make fine distinctions between levels of emotions and to put our own interpretation on how we feel. For example, one customer will say he is "disappointed" while another will feel "let down," and a third may even say she feels "betrayed"; one may say she is "delighted" while another is merely "happy"; one will experience "relief" and another "peace of mind." All such words appear regularly in conversations as customers describe their interactions with companies.

Exhibit 4.1 contains 42 words that social psychologists associate with emotions and that are routinely used by customers to describe their feelings toward companies and brands. The lists of positive and negative emotions are intended to illustrate the fact that customers' emotions may range from low intensity to high intensity. While one customer may feel contented dealing with a firm, others may express a fondness or liking for that company, while others may express enthusiasm or even use the word *love*. Many customers have told me, for example, that they *love* shopping at The Home Depot. We have actually found customers who said they were *proud* to be customers of a particular supermarket chain.

Conversely, negative emotions may range from mild annoyance or irritation, to disappointment. We routinely meet customers who *regret* having bought a particular car or who are *hurt* by an unkind comment from a salesperson. I have for some time maintained that *frustration* is the universal customer emotion because it is encountered so often. And if things get bad enough, customers will actually feel *humiliated* or *disgusted* with how they are treated.

This list of positive and negative emotions has been selected from literally hundreds of words that relate to emotions. The progression from low intensity to high intensity is somewhat arbitrary and is not intended to be scientific, but simply to illustrate the concept of a hierarchy of emotions. Also, some of the emotions may appear not to fit with others, especially as some (i.e., hatred, anger, delight, and affection) are generally directed toward an object such as a firm or brand, while others represent internal feelings (e.g., humiliation, dread, excitement, and relief). Such a distinction clearly reflects the fact that certain actions on the part of a firm result in

Exhibit 4.1   Intensity of Customer Emotions

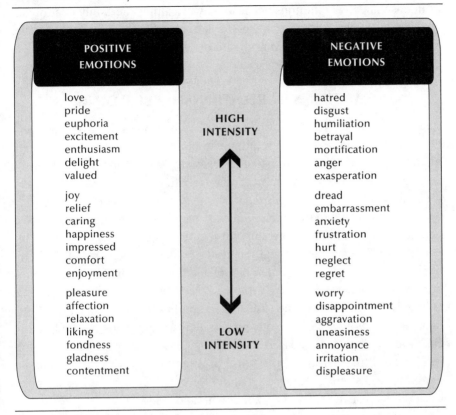

feelings *toward* the company, while others *make* a customer feel a certain way. Both are important emotional responses.

Other feelings often associated with emotions are actually bidirectional in nature: for example, concepts like surprise, amazement, and astonishment. Customers often indicate that they are surprised by something a firm or an employee does, but that surprise may be either positive or negative; the customer is pleasantly surprised or the opposite. We may be amazed at how quickly something is done or by how long it is taking. The element of surprise, while central to the creation of emotions and therefore to the building of customer relationships, is not an emotion itself but leads to the creation of positive or negative emotions.

The concept of intensity of emotions is critical to our understanding of customer relationships simply because we need to understand how important it is to create the most intense positive emotions possible so as to cement customer relationships. Likewise, we need to avoid at all costs the creation of intense negative emotions because they are almost certainly deal breakers. Few customers will willingly go back to companies with which they are disgusted or where they are humiliated or embarrassed.

EMOTIONS IN RELATIONSHIP BUILDING

The creation of positive emotions and the reduction of negative ones represent central components of relationship building. An integral component of your customer strategy must be to assess the nature and intensity of the emotions that you and your employees are creating with your customers. It is useful at this stage to revisit our model of the *drivers* of customer relationship building. It is futile to think that you can create lasting relationships unless you are successful in creating some of the more intense positive emotions.

Earlier it was observed that the kind of value created up to Level 3 of our model is largely functional in nature and that emotional value is created principally at Levels 4 and 5. Customer expectations, therefore, are defined in largely functional terms up to and including Level 3. If those largely functional expectations are met, relatively low-intensity emotions are produced—customers feel content, pleased, and may begin to develop a certain comfort level toward the firm or even a sense of affection or liking. But it takes a more focused strategy at Levels 4 and 5 to produce the more intense positive emotions such as delight, excitement, and pride.

Negative emotions are more interesting, and potentially more volatile and dangerous. Because expectations at the first three levels of our model are largely functional in nature, customers tend to take them for granted: Products will work, deliveries will arrive on time, and bills will contain no errors. Thus, failure of the core product, of a support system, or of delivery has the potential to trigger a high-level negative response, possibly because these are minimum acceptable performance standards. It is precisely because they are expected that, when these things go wrong, the emotions that are produced may not only be negative but potentially at the higher end of the intensity scale.

Recall the discussion of passive customer expectations, where it was suggested that customer expectations are, for the most part, established at the lower three levels and exceeded in a positive direction at Levels 4 and 5, thereby leading to stronger positive emotions. If expectations are not met, even at the lowest levels, the potential exists for the creation of very negative emotions including frustration, anger, and disgust.

Level 1: The Core

As we see in Exhibit 4.2, at the first level, there is not much emotion involved. The interaction with the firm is very transactional and the emphasis should be on minimizing irritants and annoyances. A customer who receives the product she was expecting may be content but would certainly not feel any strong positive emotion like delight. But if that product fails, she may well feel disappointment or anger.

Level 2: Processes and Support

If all goes well at this level, the customer is generally pleased but, again, no strong positive emotions are elicited. Most service delivery at this level is routine and, when systems work, the customer is pleased but not impressed. If her hotel reservation has been "lost in the system," however, the frequent guest is again frustrated, angry, and maybe even disgusted with how she is being treated.

Level 3: Technical Performance

At this level, a customer expects the company to deliver on its promises. The customer expects the flight to depart on time. If it does, he is generally satisfied and even pleased. If it is delayed, his anxiety increases. If it leaves an hour late and he misses a business meeting in New York, he is likely to be annoyed. He may even take his business elsewhere.

Level 4: Interaction with the Organization

It is at this level that employees in particular have an opportunity to create more intense positive and negative emotions in customers. Individualized and personalized service makes a customer feel important and valued. We have all, unfortunately, been on the receiving end of treatment at the hands of employees that was offensive, embarrassing, or humiliating.

Level 5: Emotional Elements

The emotions elicited at this level are the strongest. If they are positive, they may lead to an emotional connection. Some companies treat their customers so well that they become enthusiastic supporters and may even suggest that they are proud to be customers. However, if their dealings are negative, there

Exhibit 4.2   Hierarchy of Customer Emotions

Stages of Customer Relationship Building	Customer Emotions
LEVEL 5: The emotional connection: How your firm or brand makes the customer feel	Higher-order positive emotions: love, pride, etc.; creates meaning; reduces negatives like disgust, humiliation, anger
LEVEL 4: Getting to know us: Interpersonal connection; where the customer meets your people; face-to-face or through technology	People-based emotions like trust, comfort, friendliness, sense of community, association; reduce frustration, embarrassment, neglect
LEVEL 3: Getting it right: Delivering on promises; meeting commitments; accuracy	Satisfaction, relief; peace of mind; reduce anxiety, disappointment, regret
LEVEL 2: Backup support: Systems and processes that enhance and support the core	Generally pleased at availability of processes; not particularly impressed unless they are unavailable
LEVEL 1: The core: The essence of what the company offers; what it makes or sells, what it does	Not much emotion involved; very transactional; minimize annoyance, irritation, worry

is little likelihood that a relationship will develop. We regularly meet customers who comment that they actually dread having to deal with certain firms because they know the experience will be a difficult one or that they were mortified at how they were treated.

WHY RELATIONSHIPS LAST

Certain central elements of relationships make them genuine relationships, as distinct from acquaintances, interactions, or mere contacts. Executives and managers must have a more complete understanding of the concept if they are setting out to establish truly meaningful relationships with customers. The central themes that characterize relationships are present in all forms of relationships, regardless of whether we are talking about relationships with family members, friends, colleagues, or customers.

Essentially, if we are to practice real CRM and develop a strategy to lead to real customer relationships, we must understand how to make that emotional connection. What is it about relationships that will cause customers to feel positive emotions toward your firm more often and negative ones less often? My research into the relationships that companies have established with their customers has led me to conclude that the strongest, most positive relationships are characterized by eight key themes. These are critical things to consider as you plan your customer strategy.

We have all experienced relationships with friends, family, spouse, or partner, so we know that relationships are extremely complex and require nurturing and management. One social psychologist explains relationship building as "a very complicated and prolonged process with many pitfalls and challenges. Relationships do not just happen; they have to be made— made to start, made to work, made to develop, kept in good working order, and preserved from going sour."[4] Relationships are never static; they are continuous processes, and every interaction has the potential to change the relationship. Once a relationship is formed, a great deal of effort must be devoted to maintaining it as a healthy, viable alliance.

Clearly, different things are important to different people in establishing and maintaining relationships with others and, it may be suggested, with companies, organizations, and brands. Different customers will want different experiences in dealing with a firm and may want to be treated in one way by a firm in one situation and differently in other settings. The challenge to companies that wish to create positive customer relationships is to learn what is important to customers in their dealing with them. In any event, and the individual differences of customers notwithstanding, these are the eight most important elements in the creation and maintenance of solid, genuine relationships:

1. **Trust.** All lasting relationships are founded on trust—if one cannot trust a relationship partner, the relationship is unlikely to continue. Customers want to deal with companies that are predictable, dependable, and reliable. They want to be able to have confidence and faith in companies that they will behave as promised. They want companies and brands on which they can rely.

2. **Commitment.** There is a long-term orientation to a genuine relationship that involves a shared wish to perpetuate the relationship. Customers like to think that a company has a commitment to them. They sense immediately when a firm is interested only in making a sale. They want companies to show an interest, to demonstrate caring and concern. For their part, customers who develop a genuine loyalty to a company or brand have also made a commitment. Customers often see that commitment as a form of investment; they may point out that "my family have been customers of yours for more than 30 years"—the implication being that they have a lot invested in the relationship and expect to be treated appropriately.

3. **Familiarity.** Customers do not enjoy being in unfamiliar territory. They feel uncomfortable and out of place. One of the most powerful indicators of whether customers will continue to deal with a company is what they refer to as "comfort level"— they simply prefer to deal with companies that they feel comfortable with or that make them feel at ease.

4. **Sharing.** I believe the notion of sharing is fundamental to customer relationships, but it gets very little attention from devotees of CRM. In interpersonal relationships, we like to associate with people with whom we have a lot in common. For the same reason, we prefer companies with which we share common goals, interest, and history: "Companies like us." Customers feel most comfortable with companies that have the same values and that remind them of positive things, companies with which they have shared experiences.

5. **Communication.** When the partners in a relationship do not hear regularly from one another or when the communication is only one way, the relationship is on rocky ground. Communication must be ongoing, two way, and meaningful. Responsiveness is also an important part of communication. Customers are highly critical of companies

that never return their calls or e-mails and from which they hear "only when they want to sell me something."

6. **Liking/Attachment.** It is trite to suggest that people like to deal with people they like, but it's true. Liking and a sense of attachment is a central element of close relationships. Customers prefer to deal with companies and employees who are sincere and genuine, who recognize them and demonstrate knowledge of them and their families. One of the strongest indicators of customer loyalty is when a customer says, "They know me there." This implies a personalization of the relationship.

7. **Community.** Successful relationship builders create a sense of community among their customers. They bring customers together and make them feel part of something. They get their customers involved in the provision of service or in an active participatory role. They create a sense of "we're all in this together," that we are members of something. In many cases, companies with strong customer relationships provide a sense of support.

8. **Reciprocity.** Closely related to the notion of sharing is a sense of reciprocity; that the relationship is going to benefit both parties more or less equally. No one enjoys feeling that a relationship is one-sided, that it's all about *your* success, not mine. When a customer demonstrates loyalty to a company, a certain acknowledgment and appreciation is expected in return. The customer relationship, if it is to be a real relationship, must cut both ways. The customer must *feel* that her contribution to the relationship is recognized and welcomed.

Just as you need to regularly examine the extent to which your company and its employees are creating positive and negative emotions in your customers, you also need to think about how you can engender these eight central themes in your relationships with your customers.

HOW CAN YOU MEAN SOMETHING SPECIAL TO THEM?

Customers feel much closer to some companies and brands than to others.[5] Some occupy a central place in their lives; they come to "mean" something special to them—with the implication being that there would be a void created if the company or brand were no longer available. To "mean" something special to customers is to occupy a special place in their hearts and minds, to be *more than just a supplier of* _____. This implies the addition of certain forms of value that transcend the provision of the core product or service and is much more than simply delivering great service. The company or brand becomes a partner, an integral part of the customer's life.

The more meaningful a relationship is to a customer, the stronger will be the emotional bond. I view "meaning" as the highest form of emotional value. Acquiring meaning takes time, and in some cases results in loyalty that lasts a lifetime. Restaurants, retail stores, and brands of clothing and food products for some customers take on special meaning, relevance, and centrality in their lives. Most of us can think of relatively few firms or brands that have achieved such status. Our connection to most brands is less meaningful and in many cases borders on meaningless. The challenge in your business is to come to mean something special to as many of your customers as possible.

The meaning that your brand has for your customers resides not in the brand or the firm itself but in the minds of the customers. This is a very individualized and personal kind of meaning. I'm not talking here about how advertising depicts a brand or even about what consensus might exist about the characteristics or personality of that brand and what it "stands for." For example, brands such as Nike and Harley-Davidson have invested millions in presenting their brands in a certain light, and there is now widespread agreement on what those brands represent or stand for. But that's not what I'm referring to as the meaning in a brand.

There can be no broad consensus about what a brand means. To its most loyal customers, it is a personal thing, relating to how central a role it plays in their lives. It is a meaning that is internalized by the consumer based on how closely the brand or company fits with his values and with the things that are important to him. The brand or the firm, in fact, becomes part of how those customers define themselves.

Where meaningful relationships exist, customers speak of having a certain comfort level while shopping at *their* supermarket, of enjoying a chat with the salespeople, and of feeling relaxed. Where meaning exists in the relationship, a higher form of value has been created for the customer. The relationship takes on a status that transcends good quality, variety, service, and dependability—all of which are critically important but are increasingly taking on the status of "table stakes."

People and entities to which we feel closest and that mean the most to us are generally those with which we have a great deal in common, those with which we share a common history, values, interests, culture, and beliefs. A company or brand often means more to customers with whom it shares things. They have roots in the same community. They are interested in the same activities. They subscribe to the same values. They share meaning.

BUILDING BLOCKS OF CUSTOMER STRATEGY

Keep in mind that you need to make an emotional connection with your customers, to build on the characteristics of genuine relationships, to strike the right emotional chords. Consider the kinds of emotions you want to create and those you want to avoid, and how you will embody the characteristics of strong customer relationships as you begin to form the building blocks of your customer strategy.

The 12 principles that follow are central components that you will need to build into your customer strategy. Each involves a combination of the fundamentals of relationship building, including the positive emotions that we wish to stimulate and the negatives we must avoid. We will expand on them in the remaining chapters and provide more detail on execution in Chapter 10.

1. **Demonstrate that you appreciate their business.** Many firms appear not to recognize the fact that loyal customers are integral to their future and that without them, there is no future. They seem to take their customers (even their best customers) for granted. This implies a failure to recognize the business that these customers bring in and that they have been driving revenues for years.

   I'm not talking here about the need to establish a customer "loyalty program," which has little to do with genuine loyalty, designed as they typically are to reward repeat behavior. I'm talking more about the recognition by business that some customers have been giving us their business for a long time and showing that we not only recognize that fact but appreciate it.

2. **Earn their trust, be consistent, dependable, and reliable.** There is a great deal to say for dependability and reliability, for delivering consistently good service. If a firm delivers spotty service, gets it right only occasionally, customers will soon seek out others. I regularly encounter customers who voice their frustration and can recount stories of how they have had to switch dry cleaners, auto mechanics, or painting contractors in their often futile search for competence.

   This sounds so basic: Just get the fundamentals right and they'll come back. In some cities, in some industries, it's just not that difficult to rise above the pack. This is a basic premise: Get the basics right and you stand a chance to build a relationship. Consistently (or inconsistently) get them wrong, and customers will move on. When I ask customers why they continue to go back to certain firms again and again, the most frequently heard response is "I can always count on them to _____."

3. **Single them out for attention, personalize, customize.** No one likes to be "treated like a number," and yet customers routinely use that very expression to describe how they are made to feel in their dealings with certain companies. The more your employees can add personal touches to the interaction with customers, the more likely it is that customers will feel less like a number and more like a person. That's why young mothers love it when salespeople pay attention to their children.

   Your employees are central to your ability to personalize the interaction because this approach to relationship building so often comes across as artificial or insincere. Employees are the front line when it comes to being personal. That's why hiring for personality is so important. Customers like to deal with genuinely friendly, helpful, and personable employees. Don't hire too hastily, and hire for the best fit. Hiring is the most important relationship building decision you will make.

4. **Partner with them, help them achieve and accomplish.** Remember that what you sell and what you do represents merely a means to an end for your customers. Every one of your customers is trying to achieve certain things in her life, and you and your company can contribute to the achievement of some of those things. You should always strive to play the role of partner, which means that you have to understand just what customers are facing, what they are trying to accomplish, and the context in which they are operating.

   Customers appreciate input from companies that understand what they are going through, can empathize with them, and can come up with solutions. They can immediately sense whether a company understands and cares. In a business-to-business setting, there is no more damning client comment than "You really don't understand my business." Businesses must constantly strive not only to understand but to contribute to the success of their customers and to help them look good in the eyes of those whom they are trying to impress. The comment you want to hear from customers is "I couldn't have done it without you."

5. **Create customer involvement; build communities.** Customers feel closer to companies with which they have some form of interaction. They enjoy being more active, as opposed to passive, recipients of

whatever the company directs at them. No one enjoys being a target. Thus, make interaction a component of your customer strategy. Allow customers to interact with your company on a regular basis, through events, community sponsorships, and occasions that allow for the meeting of other customers who share the same interests.

Any components of your strategy that allow your customers to feel a part of something, to feel a sense of community, will contribute to the emotional attachment that we have been talking about. A genuine "club" feeling will provide social support for customers and contribute to shared experiences. A frequent-shopper or "loyalty" program usually doesn't accomplish this, because the emotional connection is missing.

6. **Establish effective two-way communications.** Nothing destroys a relationship more quickly than a lack of ongoing communications. Customers are quick to point out that they don't consider their interaction with many firms to be "relationships" because "I never hear from them." A fundamental expectation in relationships is that we will hear from the other party occasionally. But what we hear must be meaningful and relevant. A few years ago I had discussions with a telecommunications company that was in the process of developing its "Small and Medium Enterprise customer contact strategy." It had decided that "A" customers were to be contacted 24 times a year, "B" customers 18 times, and so on. But it had decided that the sending of the monthly bill constituted 12 contacts. To customers, receiving a bill is not a particularly personal contact.

   Components of your two-way communications package must deal with being responsive, calling them back, and returning their e-mails. One of the comments that I hear very frequently from customers is "They never call me back; they are obviously not interested in my business."

7. **Share things with your customers.** People like to spend time with others with whom they have a lot in common. Show your customers that you have a lot in common with them. You are from the same place, grew up in the same neighborhoods, have the same values. You are committed to the things to which they are committed. A regional client of mine achieved great success in the face of competition from much larger national and international companies when it branded itself "the Home Team." Customers rallied behind the firm as it faced down the "Visitors."

But sharing also extends to things that you have or have access to that you can share with them. The Internet makes it far easier today to share news and information with selected customers and to make it a very personal experience. In a business-to-business (B2B) context, you demonstrate great interest in your client when you share with her an interesting article that you have read or an opportunity to hear a speaker on a subject of interest.

8. **Remind them of things.** Nostalgia is a very powerful emotive tool. People enjoy being reminded of pleasant occasions and experiences. You should remind your customers of occasions when you and your brand played an important role in their lives. Bring back memories that clearly associate your brand with happy events. Customers regularly associate certain companies and brands with occasions, events, accomplishments, and milestones. Brand loyalty is built on a solid foundation of recollections of what the brand made possible or situations of which it was an integral part.

When I was working on a project with Kraft Foods a few years ago, the loyalty of many customers to the Kraft brand was obvious, but so too was the number of customers whose loyalty was grounded in long-standing memories. Many made reference to the fact that they cannot think of Kraft without thinking of toasting marshmallows over a campfire on family camping trips or of making peanut butter and jelly sandwiches after school.

9. **Associate with what's central in their lives.** Believe it or not, the most important things in the lives of your customers are not your brand or the products and services that you and your competitors provide. When I ask customers what is most important to them or what they are passionate about, they seldom mention Sears or FedEx or even Starbucks. Typically, the answers start with children, family, pets, and home, and then extend to getting together with friends, music, eating properly, reading, vacations, working out, enjoying the outdoors, taking care of myself, financial planning, or a nice bottle of wine with friends over dinner.

Once you have identified what your target customers are most interested in and how they spend their time, you have great insight into the kinds of things that you can connect with so as to demonstrate that you have interests in common and that you are committed to making these things possible for them. This leads you into many logical and strategic decisions relating to events that you can organize for your clients, presentations to which you can invite them, and things that you can sponsor that will strike a chord.

10. **Piggyback on their relationships with others.** Your customers have well-established relationships with other people, groups, activities, and organizations. You should take advantage of that fact and build it into your customer strategy. These already existing relationships form the basis for a strategic approach to events, partnerships, and sponsorships. You should set out to borrow some of the meaning that these entities have already created among your customers.

    If your research shows, for example, that many of your target customers are keenly interested in golf, bridge, opera, or jazz, these represent opportunities to organize clinics, tournaments, or concerts that will appeal to them. You might sponsor a concert tour or the local appearance of Diana Krall, or Winton Marsalis, or Ben Heppner. You might decide to partner with a local florist or garden center to organize a "getting your garden ready for winter" seminar, if a large percentage of your target customers are avid gardeners. The concept of borrowed meaning forms the basis for all strategic decisions relating to partnerships, sponsorships, and the selection of spokespersons.

11. **Get rid of irritants and stupid rules.** Remember that the little things often send big messages and cause major irritation. Customers tell me that they hate it when they go to their bank to use an ATM only to find that it's out of envelopes. They are irritated when they have to complete long, detailed forms when returning unsuitable items at retail stores. They are bothered when the magazines in waiting areas are months, if not years, old.

    Every company has rules for its employees and customers to follow that appear to the customers to be absolutely stupid. They exist for no obvious reason or are designed clearly to benefit the company and not its customers. I was in the first-class airport lounge of a major European airline on a Sunday morning recently, on my way to London. The large lounge was practically empty, with only me and one other customer enjoying a coffee and the Sunday papers. A gold-card customer of the airline was denied entry to the lounge that morning because he was accompanied by his wife and teenage daughter. It was explained most emphatically to him that the rules clearly state that each member is permitted only one guest. A stupid rule? Not on a Friday afternoon when the lounge is full of business travelers on their way home for the weekend. But on a Sunday morning when the lounge is practically empty?

12. **Surprise them every now and then.** The element of surprise represents a major opportunity to impress, begin or cement a relationship, and stimulate positive conversation. There are numerous opportunities every day to impress customers by doing things that they simply are not expecting. Practice "planned spontaneity," which is the act of appearing spontaneous to your customers while having a plan and a culture in place to watch for opportunities to surprise. It's all about training and encouraging your employees to constantly seek opportunities to impress. It's about behaving outside that conventional box by doing things customers aren't expecting of you.

Planned spontaneity means having your employees regularly saying to customers "Let us look after that for you." This sends a powerful message that not only do we understand what you are going through but we care enough about you to take care of it, even though it's not what you would normally expect of us. My favorite planned spontaneity story involves the bellman at a Delta Hotel who offered to dry my running clothes for me when I returned from a late-afternoon run in a winter rainstorm. He not only had the clothing dried, it was washed and ironed and placed in a neat pile at the foot of my bed!

Endnotes

1. Carolyn Leitch, "Best Buy's Secret: Sales Staff," *The Globe and Mail,* June 17, 2005, p. B12.

2. Leonard L. Berry, "Relationship Marketing," in *Emerging Perspectives on Services Marketing,* ed. Leonard L. Berry, G. Lynn Shostack, and Gregory D. Upah (Chicago: American Marketing Association, 1983), pp. 25–28.

3. For example, see S. S. Kleine, R. E. Kleine III, and C. T. Allen, "How is a possession 'me' or 'not me'? Characterizing types and an antecedent of material possession attachment," *Journal of Consumer Research,* 22, December, (1995), 327–343; Grant McCracken, "Culture and consumption: a theoretical account of the structure and movement of the cultural meaning of consumer goods," *Journal of Consumer Research,* 13 June, (1986), 71–84; and Melanie Wallendorf and Eric J. Arnould, "My favorite things: a cross-cultural inquiry into object attachment, possessiveness, and social linkages," *Journal of Consumer Research,* 15, March, (1988), 532–546.

4. Steve Duck, *Understanding Relationships* (New York: Guilford Press, 1991), p. 3.

5. For a more detailed examination of the concept of meaning in customer relationships, see James G. Barnes, "Establishing Meaningful Customer Relationships: Why Some Companies and Brands Mean More to Their Customers," *Managing Service Quality* 13, no. 3 (2003): 178–186.

5

BEYOND MUNDANE EXPERIENCES

Another subject on which everyone seems to have an opinion these days is the *customer experience*. Many seem to have just discovered it, as if it's something new. It isn't. Whether you realize it or not, every time a customer deals with you, he is having an experience. It may not be an *experience* in the way that some authors approach the subject—as in an exciting, entertaining, memorable experience—but it *is* an experience nonetheless.

All experiences have the potential to elicit responses from customers. Think about when you have experienced (there's that word again!) very poor service from a company and how you felt and responded as a result. Think also about a situation when a company impressed you with how it handled a certain situation and how you felt afterward. Customer experiences, of all kinds, have the potential to produce emotional responses. That is why we are dealing with them here, because they are so important.

Executives now seem to realize just how important the customer experience is in influencing customer satisfaction and loyalty. There is a widespread acceptance of the fact that conventional elements of the so-called marketing mix no longer have the ability to set a company apart from its competitors. In a study conducted in the United Kingdom, Colin Shaw and John Ivens of Beyond Philosophy found that 71 percent of business executives believed that the customer experience is the "next competitive battleground."[1] Further, 85 percent agreed that it is no longer sustainable to differentiate only on the physical aspects of the customer experience, such as price, quality, and delivery. But Shaw and Ivens also found that while 85 percent of business leaders thought that engaging emotionally with customers could increase loyalty, only 15 percent seem to be doing anything about it by exploring customers' emotional expectations, and only 5 percent indicated that they try to evoke a specific emotion among customers.

A study by Bain & Company in the United States found that 80 percent of companies surveyed believed that they delivered a "superior experience" to their customers. But when customers were asked to indicate their perceptions of the experiences they have in dealing with companies, they rated only 8 percent of companies as truly delivering a superior experience.[2] Do you sense just a little bit of disconnect between the companies' view of experience and that of the customers who are doing the experiencing? "Customer experience" is in grave danger of becoming yet another management buzzword that businesspeople bandy about without fully understanding its meaning or its potential.

A BROADER VIEW

As is the case with value, quality, and other principles that are central to a customer strategy, the concept of the customer experience is not a simple one. It is, in fact, very complex and multidimensional. Therefore, to speak of improving the customer experience demands that we dig deeply and actually complicate the discussion by delving into various types of experiences.

Many customer experiences are eminently forgettable. They are unimpressive simply because nothing particularly important happened. It is a challenge for a business to turn such experiences into something more than they are. We can improve on them, make them more pleasant or less taxing, but it's difficult to turn buying a newspaper or filling the tank with gasoline into a "WOW!"

But you do have opportunities every time you interact with customers to add a certain kind of value that will enhance the experience of dealing with you. Let's say you decided to rent a car for a short California vacation. I'll use this fairly ordinary example to illustrate the various components or dimensions of the customer experience. There are, potentially at least, four different experiences involved in what is, on the surface, the simple rental of a car.

You have decided to rent a car from Avis because you have used the company before and are generally pleased with its service. You will fly into San Francisco, pick up the car at the airport, spend a few days driving around the Napa Valley, then drive down the Big Sur coast, dropping the car off at Los Angeles International Airport before flying out.

Easy to Deal With

The first component of your experience is related to how easy the rental car company is to deal with. In fact, this seems to me the principal way that many managers approach the subject of the customer experience: How easy are we to deal with? This question pertains principally to the various systems and processes that Avis has in place to enable you to rent a car with a minimum of hassle. You can book the car online or by phone from a central reservations center, or you can have your travel agent do it. You can preselect the size and style of car and whether you want insurance coverage. If you are an Avis Preferred member, your car will be ready for you when you arrive; you just show your driver's license and drive away. When you drop your car off at the airport, Avis will have attendants with handheld scanning devices that print your bill right at the car, and you are ready to go to your flight in seconds. All of this falls into the area of being easy to deal with and making things as simple as possible for the customer.

Folks You Meet

When you do have an opportunity to meet and talk with employees of Avis, how do they handle the situation and deal with you? This happens if you make your reservation by calling the central reservation center, when you go to the counter at the airport to get the keys to your car, and when the attendant checks the car in at the airport. Occasionally you may talk with or meet other representatives of the company. The central question is whether these employees make the experience a positive one by being helpful, efficient, friendly, and all of the other positive attributes we associate with good customer service personnel. They are the front line in the creation of a positive customer experience. As we will see later in this chapter, the people we put in front of customers have a great deal of influence over the outcome of the experience.

Product in Use

This aspect of the broad concept of the customer experience doesn't get a lot of attention from some firms. It refers to the experience you have from the time you drive the rental car away from the airport until you return it. How can Avis enhance this part of your experience, when you are actually out of sight of the company? This is a situation faced by all companies that entertain or welcome visitors—hotels, airlines, theaters, restaurants—and it's related to the in-store experience in retailing, except in those situations the customer remains in contact with the employees of the company. The same principle also applies in all situations where customers buy tangible products: What can Nike do to enhance the experience of wearing its shoes, or Apple the use of iPods? Unfortunately, in some companies, customers are left with the feeling that they are on their own. Avis can give you a 1-800 number to call in the event that you have a problem with the car, supply you with the locations of Avis offices in the areas where you plan to travel, and ensure that there is a map, flashlight, and first aid kit in the car.

The Broader Experience

Remember that all customer purchases and interactions with firms are initiated for a reason. You are renting that car to take you into the Napa Valley and down the coast to Los Angeles. The car is, quite simply, a means to a greater end—you need a car to get where you want to go. But what if Avis were more than simply the company that supplies you with a car? If it knew a little bit more about your plans, it could become an important contributor to your enjoying a getaway to Napa and Big Sur. It could point out places to see, wineries that are not to be missed, or provide a CD that offers you a guided tour of Carmel and Monterey. If it sees that you are traveling with children, it might supply games they can play to while away the drive time. The more that Avis knows about you and the purpose of your trip, the more it can customize the experience to enhance your enjoyment and your image of the company.

BACK TO RELATIONSHIP BUILDING

The customer experience offers your firm a tremendous opportunity to differentiate yourself. Lots of business is lost because of bad customer experiences. And the frequency of experiences is so vast that there are many opportunities every day to impress customers or to mess up.

The customer experience is one of the central pillars in the building of customer relationships and, therefore, a fundamental component of a customer strategy. You should be constantly asking yourself how well you are doing in offering the most positive experience possible to your customers. If we go back to our five-level model of customer relationship building (see Exhibit 5.1), we can see how the offering of progressively more impressive customer experiences can contribute to the development of lasting, emotion-driven customer relationships. The experience plays a major role at each stage of relationship development.

Level 1: The Core

At this stage, the experience is all about having the basics available. It may not constitute more than a simple exchange. Things go well; the core is available,

Exhibit 5.1   Levels of Customer Experience

Stages of Customer Relationship Building	Customer Experiences
LEVEL 5: The emotional connection: How your firm or brand makes the customer feel	Transcends what the firm typically does; addresses what it contributes to, makes possible
LEVEL 4: Getting to know us: Interpersonal connection; where the customer meets your people; face-to-face or through technology	Employees important in creating positive experience, customization, personalization, ambiance, facilitation
LEVEL 3: Getting it right: Delivering on promises; meeting commitments; accuracy	Everything according to plan, no surprises; service is delivered as promised
LEVEL 2: Backup support: Systems and processes that enhance and support the core	Interaction often with technology; impersonal, emphasis on being easy to do business with; in the zone
LEVEL 1: The core: The essence of what the company offers; what it makes or sells, what it does	Very basic; very little interaction may be involved; product and service availability

appropriately priced, and of reasonable quality. Service is quick and efficient but hardly memorable. The technology works as it should. Such experiences occur many times a day and, unless something goes horribly wrong, they are difficult to recall by the time evening comes. The key from the firm's perspective is to make sure that things don't go off the rails.

Level 2: Backup Support

The customer experience at this stage is all about being easy to deal with: making sure that systems work, that service is available 24/7, and that offices are conveniently available and open during hours that meet customer needs. It's all about minimizing the number of hoops through which we ask customers to jump and the amount of work we foist on to them. It's putting the appropriate technology in place and sufficient numbers of employees to get the job done quickly and efficiently, and with a minimum of customer frustration being caused. Occasionally, companies can create a "WOW!" by being much easier to deal with than the competition, but such advantages are usually copied quickly.

Level 3: Getting It Right

In some industries and businesses, customer expectations are so low that simply getting things right—delivering on time, fixing things the first time, showing up when they said they would—represents a positive customer experience. Generally, it is quite fashionable to complain about service, to the point where many customers are positively impressed when a company meets its promises. Of course, some companies that have been able to create a culture and systems that support superior performance have turned this into a competitive advantage. FedEx and Nordstrom come to mind.

You may have noted that, to this point, the progression of customer experience as an important contributor to relationship building has been largely reactive, in the sense that the firm tries to ensure that nothing goes wrong to create a *bad* experience. We now turn to those aspects of the customer experience that may actually exceed expectations and create surprisingly positive experiences through proactivity.

Level 4: Getting to Know Us

The greater the interpersonal interaction between customers and your employees, the greater the potential to enhance the customer experience through surprisingly good service and the customization of the interaction.

We have all had experiences that were made special because of the initiative taken by an individual employee. We all know of companies whose reputation is based on the quality of people they employ and their devotion to the customer. We all probably can think of companies to which we go back again and again simply because of how we are treated by an individual employee. Your people have the best opportunity to enhance customer experiences, especially in service environments where they meet and talk with customers.

Level 5: The Emotional Connection

At this stage of the customer experience model, you have the opportunity to take the notion of an experience to another level. Here's where you *create* experiences rather than simply enhancing or contributing to them. Again, I'm not talking about turning every customer encounter into a circus performance or a half-time show, I'm taking about doing things that create *meaningful* value for your customers and that will impress them simply because they appreciate that you've taken the time and made the effort to deliver. This demands a great deal of outside-the-box thinking and some creativity, both of which we will tackle in the next chapter.

NOW THEY ARE EXPERIENCES

In an earlier time, we would have referred to customer experiences as encounters or interactions. Just because some people now refer to them as experiences does not mean that they have taken on more relevance in recent years. The simple fact of the matter is that most interactions that customers have with companies go rather well. Most purchase situations that you and I engage in as customers, and many business-to-business (B2B) interactions in fact, are unspectacular, simply because so little is at stake. They are rather ordinary, there is little that can go wrong to ruin the day, and there is little risk involved. What most of us hope for in such situations is that nothing *will* go wrong and that the interaction or transaction is completed with little hassle or delay. And most are.

As is often pointed out in the context of advertising, most of us, just before our heads hit the pillow at the end of a long day, are unable to remember more than five or six of the thousands of advertising messages to which we have been exposed during the preceding 15 or 16 hours. We have fewer, but still a very large number of, interactions or experiences with businesses and other organizations during the course of a day. Similarly, most pass without comment or even notice, and we certainly would not consider them memorable.

That is how it should be for most customer experiences. Nothing happens. The product is in stock, you find it easily, the price is okay, the sales clerk is available and efficient, the line at the checkout is fairly short and moves quickly, and you found a parking spot close to the door. What more could you want?

For encounters such as these, and their online equivalents, businesses should make it as easy as possible for customers to complete the interaction as efficiently and in as pleasant an environment as possible. The focus is on the functional side—make sure things go well and that you *are* easy to deal with.

This is a sort of passive view of experience creation. Make sure things don't go wrong. Make it simple and easy. But there is an important proactive side to the discussion on experiences. We should look for opportunities to enhance certain experiences (not all) and elevate them beyond the mundane.

CENTRAL TO STRATEGY DEVELOPMENT

The customer experience offers an opportunity to add a certain kind of value (in fact, many kinds) and to contribute to the creation of positive customer emotions and the reduction of negative ones. In that sense, it is fundamentally important to the creation of the right kind of responses from customers, to the development of satisfaction, and ultimately to loyalty. If you offer customers bad experiences often enough, chances are they'll eventually stop coming.

We need to understand what aspects of the customer experience drive certain emotions. What can we do that will impress and cause customers to tell their friends? What might we be doing that causes them frustration, anxiety, or other negative emotions? What should we do to ensure that negative emotions do not result from the way customers are handled?

The customer experience must be appropriate to the customer and to the setting in which the customer is operating; as mentioned, all experiences do not have the potential to be turned into memorable events. But all do have the potential to affect whether the customer will be back again and whether she feels comfortable and happy dealing with your firm. So you need to think constantly about what the customer is experiencing when dealing with you. It's more than what we generally refer to as "service"; that's only one part of the experience. More important is how the customer feels.

EXPERIENCE IS NOT (USUALLY) ENTERTAINMENT

Some who have written about customer experiences in recent years seem to be of the opinion that all customer interaction has the potential to create a "WOW!" moment for the customer. Joseph Pine and James Gilmore, who coined the concept of the "experience economy," are especially guilty of perpetuating that view that all customer experiences should be fun, engaging, and entertaining.[3] They talk about selecting themes, performing on stages, employees as performers with props, and so on. These things are all very well and good, and indeed important, when the customer is seeking a fun and entertaining time. If I go to Disney World or Hard Rock Café with family or friends, I expect a good time, but I don't expect or demand a good time from a supermarket or a business hotel. I do expect things to go smoothly, and I will appreciate it if I am pleasantly surprised by something they thought to do that enhances the experience, but I don't have to be entertained while buying groceries. In fact, in such situations the addition of an entertainment component to the experience is positively irritating and distracting for some customers.

Some organizations feel that their customers have to be exposed to some form of entertainment wherever they go. Many restaurants have big-screen televisions, CNN and the NBA are inescapable, airline flight attendants think they are Seinfeld, and waiters think they can and must sing. But not every customer experience requires marching bands, big-screen television, and singing wait staff.

The kind of customer experience you create, and the degree to which it is characterized as entertainment, depends on a number of factors, not least of which are your company or brand positioning, the setting, and the target segments to whom you wish to appeal.

THE BRAND EXPERIENCE

Your company or brand is often an integral part of the customer experience. This means that your role involves much more than simply providing a great product at a great price and also embodies how customers feel about making your company or brand a part of their experience. We see this when customers refer to brands that are a central feature in their occasions: "It isn't Thanksgiving at our home without a Butterball turkey." "A picnic on the beach isn't complete without Kraft marshmallows." In other words, the customer is saying that the brand is a central component of the experience.

How do you make your brand a more central part of the occasion, an essential contributor? How do we move to playing a meaningful, rather than a superficial, role? David Norton of Yamamoto Moss, a Minneapolis-based brand strategy firm, suggests that consumers (and consumption) have changed in the past 20 years and that they are now looking for meaningful brand experiences.[4] He argues that we moved during the 1990s from consuming things to consuming experiences. I would add that many of those experiences, as they became more easily accessed, also became increasingly superficial and meaningless. For many companies, theme parks, Legolands and Niketowns came to define the concept of the customer experience, and many customers have found them lacking in anything approaching meaning.

What is missing in many brand experiences, especially those that are grounded in a sense of entertainment, is what Norton refers to as "cultural capital"—the intangible benefits that are associated with life events. Quoting the sociologist Pierre Bourdieu, Norton explains that meaningful experiences cannot be bought but can only be accumulated through acts of kindness, giving, service, and other social mechanisms that lead to the creation of cultural capital. They are, as MasterCard has been pointing out to us for years, literally priceless.

To be meaningful, brands have to stand for something, to have an essence that is relevant to the accomplishment of something of value, to contribute to successful outcomes, to genuinely care. The best brands are those that send the message that they know their customers and what they are trying to accomplish in life, and that they are committed to helping them along the way. This is a long way away from having great products and trying to sell customers more of them.

What do these meaningful brands stand for and make possible? The key to the creation of meaningful brand experience is to be very clear on what your brand stands for and to create situations where customers can have such experiences. As exemplified in its tagline "Relax, it's FedEx," Federal Express stands for peace of mind—if you really want that package to be in Des Moines by 10:30 tomorrow, there really is no choice. Howard Schultz, chairman of Starbucks, decided many years ago that Starbucks' positioning and what it means to its loyal customers has less to do with coffee than it does with being that "third place" in people's lives: the place that fosters a sense of community between home and the workplace.

Four Seasons sets out to create a hotel experience that is dedicated to the highest standards of hospitality, a sense of luxury for those who know and appreciate the best. The culture of that company is all about creating memorable experiences. Tesco is more than a supermarket; Harrods is more than a department store; and IKEA is more than a furniture retailer—not because of the products that each sells, but because of the different experiences that each creates. Tesco offers a Wine Club and a healthy living component on their Web site. Harrods exemplifies luxury shopping, to the point where tourists flock to afternoon tea and proudly tote their shopping bags to the local supermarket when they get home. IKEA offers children's play areas to make the shopping experience a bit more enjoyable for all family members. These companies live their brand values.

WHAT CONTRIBUTES TO THE EXPERIENCE?

Many things contribute to the customer experience. The concept is, in fact, extremely complex. Many companies fail to appreciate just how complex and tend to have a fairly simplistic view of the customer experience as a result. Fundamental to a successful outcome from a customer experience is having the basics available and getting them right. Much customer frustration results from finding that what should be taken for granted is not available. Customers leave when items are out of stock and when they can't get served.

Also, don't underestimate the importance of what customers call the "little things." Because you are so close to your business, you and your staff often do not see what the customer sees. Little things become irritants or detract from the image you are trying to portray and the service the customer wants. Why should a customer with a two-year-old and an infant have to walk to the center of a shopping mall to find the "customer service" center where she can rent kiddie carts? A Volvo dealership recently changed hands and is now owned by a company that also represents Nissan. For months after the changeover, Volvo customers, when they called the dealership and were put on hold, had to listen to Nissan messages and commercials. An irritant, a little thing—but many customers noticed and mentioned it.

The physical space in which the service is delivered is also an important contributor to the customer experience. In fact, if the physical appearance and "feel" of your offices and retail space are not pleasant and welcoming, customers may not even bother entering into an experience. Don't underestimate the importance of first impressions. Boxes left in aisles and corridors, windows that haven't been washed, torn carpet: All send the message that the company doesn't care. They also raise questions in the minds of customers about the kind of service they are likely to receive. The design of that physical space is also important. Women have commented regularly to me in focus groups that they don't enjoy shopping for clothing in stores where the mirrors are *outside* the changing rooms. Seniors comment that they would like some place to sit down for a few minutes while pushing that heavy shopping cart around the supermarket.

Your systems with which customers come into contact, your various rules and regulations that govern interaction with customers, all affect their reaction to the experience of dealing with you. Customers around the world are frustrated by poorly designed interactive voice response (IVR) telephone systems—you know, the "press 1 for billing, press 2 for sales, press 3 for customer service" systems. They are doubly frustrated by those that implore them every now and then to stay on the line because their call is "very important to us." Does nobody sense the irony in this situation? Customers certainly do and regularly hang up. If the call was truly important to the company, it would have been answered promptly.

You would be well advised to review all systems with which your customers come into contact, the various rules to which they have to adhere, and the hoops through which they have to jump in order to deal with you. You may not see them as barriers or impediments, but your customers certainly do. You can likely explain why they have to be there and the savings you realize by having them in place. But my experience suggests that they represent a formidable barrier to customer relationship building. They are one of the most important causes of the "almost customer" phenomenon, which we will discuss in Chapter 8.

In many cases, it is your people who have the most important impact on the customer experience. Customers routinely comment on how well they were treated (or how poorly) and that this is a primary reason for their going back to deal with a company again (or not). Customers can sense right away whether your employees enjoy their jobs, whether they really are committed to their customers. Their attitude and body language send loud messages to customers. When supermarket shoppers are asked why they continue to shop at their regular supermarket, many mention the fact that employees, when they ask them where to find the pickles, will actually lead them to their location rather than pointing them to aisle 19.

This is why I often suggest to managers and executives that the human resources side of their business demands their attention, simply because the people whom you put in front of customers are of such critical importance in creating the right atmosphere and experience. Hiring is an extremely important decision—some people are just nice folks, are naturally pleasant and friendly, and enjoy dealing with people. Others are not. Even how you compensate your employees will have an impact on whether customers enjoy their experience. I am increasingly hearing from customers that they are uncomfortable shopping in retail stores where the staff is paid on commission.

Customers walk out because they don't like situations where they feel pressured to buy.

ELEVATING THE EXPERIENCE BEYOND THE MUNDANE

There are certain situations where it is appropriate to add something special, something beyond the expected to make the customer experience a memorable one. Some such situations are obvious because many special occasions are easily identified—milestones like a wedding, graduation from college, job promotion, or the birth of a child. That's why a travel agent will send a couple a bottle of champagne when they leave port on a cruise to celebrate their twenty-fifth wedding anniversary.

But enhancing an experience doesn't have to involve a special occasion; it may involve making an occasion special. For example, some companies occasionally recognize loyal customers. For many years, my wife and I were very regular customers of a certain Mexican restaurant. One evening, we dropped in for dinner, were shown to our "regular" table, and literally before we had settled into our seats our server brought a glass of sangria for my wife and a Corona for me. When we expressed our surprise and explained that we hadn't ordered these drinks, our server said, "Yes, but you always do. These are on the house tonight because you are such great customers."

Think also about experiences that may have been special at one time but that have become mundane over time. For example, in the B2B context, many firms continue to try to add value for their customers by inviting them to participate in social occasions: They take them to dinner, invite them to hockey or basketball games or to play golf. This form of competitive activity has become such a commonplace event that it has lost its special feel. More and more businesspeople are turning down such invitations because they realize that they have little to do with business. Some companies have concluded that such invitations become taken for granted after a time and have little differentiating effect. As a result, they have dramatically reduced their involvement. The pharmaceutical industry no longer allows its members to engage in such activities. The challenge is to turn what has become mundane into the business-building opportunity it was intended to be.

Take, for example, the annual "golf day" to which some businesses have been inviting their customers for years. In my experience, such events have become quite commonplace and no longer are seen to be special in any way. Regular golfers are often not interested because they can play golf whenever they want; why leave the office for a day to play golf with strangers whose company they may not even enjoy? Many well-intentioned companies whose objective of showing appreciation to their better customers is admirable have seen participation in their annual golf day dropping off in recent years. The issue is one of trying to restore such events to special status or to move on to something else that will have an element of surprise and will set the firm apart.

I talked recently with a Lexus dealer who has encountered exactly this drop in participation in an annual golf event. I suggested that the dealership take a strategic look at what it was trying to accomplish. While showing your customers that you appreciate their business is a commendable objective, there are much more creative ways to accomplish this than simply inviting them to play golf. Presumably, there would also be some business development objectives, yet this firm was inviting to the golf day only people who already drive a Lexus.

I proposed a variation on the golf theme, one that will require some strategizing and a little more effort but should address some different objectives, reach prospective customers, and generally be more enjoyable for participants. I suggested that the Lexus dealer identify a smaller number of loyal customers to invite to a different kind of golf day, one where the Lexus owner would create his own foursome. Customers should be selected for their position in the community and their sphere of influence. By inviting them to build their own foursome, the Lexus dealer is changing the format and feel of the conventional golf day, customizing the event, and asking its best customers to invite friends or business associates to participate, many or most of whom will be driving competing makes of cars.

Personalization, customization, and recognition are key concepts in creating customer experiences that stand out from the mundane.

PERSONALIZING THE CUSTOMER EXPERIENCE

Any attempt to personalize an experience has to involve *appropriate* personalization. Not all customer experiences can or should be personal ones. We should also make an important distinction between "getting personal" and personalizing the experience. Mundane, daily occurrences should be pleasant, efficient, friendly but not necessarily personal. I disagree that all experiences should become personal. In fact, some customers will find it too intrusive if we try to get too close. Remember, many people just want to do their banking or grocery shopping as efficiently as possible. Let's not try to make some experiences more than they are.

There's an important difference between getting personal and customizing the experience so that the customer feels as if special attention is being paid to her. The notion of "fit" is very important here. You and your employees should pay attention to the idea of fitting the product or service to the unique needs or characteristics of the customer. By doing so, you send the message that you have noticed or learned something important and are tailoring the product or service as a result.

The degree or extent of personalization is important. How far do we go? And how do we implement a personalization component to our customer strategy when some people don't want us to get too close? We need to decide just what personalization means and when to play that card.

Some product categories simply lend themselves to personalization and to the notion of "fit," yet many companies simply do not take advantage of this fact. Take mattresses, for example. A mattress is an innately personal product, one that most customers will use for years and one with which they have very close contact, unlike many products that we buy. The notion of fit or customization is especially important in mattresses, simply because of the importance of a good night's sleep. Mattresses also are products about which customers will use what is very emotive language. Frequent travelers will, for example, often comment on how good it feels to "get home to my own bed." Why is it, then, that mattress retailers typically ask the same questions when customers come into the store. One recently told me that he asks customers whether they prefer a hard or soft mattress and roughly how much they plan to spend. How impersonal; all about the product, nothing about a great night's sleep.

One company that does realize the personalization possibilities of mattresses is Kingsdown, a Mebane, North Carolina–based manufacturer with plants across the United States and Canada that has been making mattresses since 1904. Kingsdown talks about mattresses as a means to an end—a great night's sleep. The company has invested in research and development to come up with its DormoDiagnostic system to custom-fit a customer to a mattress. Customers can either lie on a diagnostic bed at a Kingsdown retailer, and have the bed record certain measurements and recommend the "right" mattress, or they can complete a virtual assessment online. The Kingsdown online system records basic body measurements (height, weight, waist size) and demographics such as age and gender. It also asks if customers suffer from arthritis or experience pain in various parts of their bodies.

This is a start at customization. I'd take the personalization of the mattress-buying experience to another level. For most customers, a mattress is a mystery. They know little or nothing about the construction, what coil count is all about, or what mattress will actually deliver that great night's sleep. The customer needs help and needs to be made to feel that she is being fitted to the best mattress to meet her needs. I'd ask a lot more questions about how many hours of sleep the customer likes to get each night, how many days a year she is away from home, whether she sleeps on her back or side. The point of such questions is not only to fit the customer to the best mattress, but to *demonstrate* that we are doing so. By asking such questions, we send the message that we know sleep and the factors that lead to a customer experiencing the great night's sleep that everyone wants.

SCRIPTS AND SYSTEMS—NOT PERSONAL!

Some things that are touted as personalization really aren't. Customers find the phrase, "Did you find everything you were looking for?" not as a genuine inquiry but rather as an attempt to sell them just one more thing before they exit the store. Calling a customer by name when her name pops up on a screen is not genuine personalization.

I find it a strange view of customer relationship building to assume that databases and systems have to be relied on to create personal experiences. And yet that is what is going on in many companies, where large investments have been made in databases and data mining systems. A specific occasion, such as the purchase of a certain product or a request for an address change, triggers what is now called "dialogue marketing" that prompts some communication from the firm to the customer, usually containing a special offer or the announcement of a new product.[5] Although I cannot argue with the notion that certain life events trigger specific customer needs and that companies that are aware of such events can then personalize the experience, I am less comfortable with the idea that a "system" generates the communication with the customer and that the message is usually, as the customer will observe, aimed at selling him something.

Having the "system" send me a reminder note is not personal, or at least not as personal as a company can be if its employees are sensitive to opportunities to impress customers. Your employees have the potential to create and embellish customer experiences by offering truly personalized solutions and initiatives. These solutions are especially important in companies that do not have the technology and systems necessary to maintain customer databases and to capture data on an ongoing basis. But they are also important in that they can add an element of emotional value in ways that systems-generated messages never can, as we will see in the examples that follow.

The same argument applies to the use of scripts by contact center and other employees. The mere fact that a company is employing scripts to guide what employees should say in certain situations suggests a stifling of creativity, that we can pigeonhole customer experiences into a certain set of categories, each of which warrants a certain conversation. So much for customization! I viewed it as a good sign, therefore, when I read in early 2006 that Lloyds TSB, a major U.K. bank, had decided to eliminate scripts from their call centers, based on research that indicated that 90 percent of customers are annoyed when they are talking to call center employees who are obviously reading from a prepared script.[6] Half of those interviewed said they thought the use of scripts is really impersonal.

RECOGNIZING LIFE EVENTS: THE CONCEPT OF GRADUATION

Most companies miss a great many opportunities to create customer experiences that would be meaningful and, therefore, emotionally valued. Think about the fact that individuals and families experience a series of often predictable events as they progress through life. Many of these may be foreseen and captured in a customer profile or database: birthdays, anniversaries, anticipated date of graduation from college, and so on. Such events represent the low-hanging fruit. Many companies instinctively take the opportunity to offer congratulations, when in fact the customer perceives them as artificial rather than genuine. Why would my car dealer send me a birthday card; especially when I know the card was issued by "the system" simply because they "captured" my birth date from my driver's license when I bought the car?

I believe there is tremendous potential in focusing your customer strategy on life events that are not publicly known and that generally escape the attention of database marketers and others who are attempting to enhance a customer relationship. We all experience such events, and they occur on a regular basis. They may be cause for private celebration within a close group of family and friends but rarely become public knowledge. Yet they are of considerable importance in marking stages of life as we pass through them. They are a big deal to those experiencing them. Photographs are taken and sent to family members; they are the content of family photo albums and scrapbooks. They also represent occasions that, if recognized and acknowledged by your business, will surprise and impress customers.

The purchase of certain items signifies the passage of time and the moving to another life stage. Decorating a nursery, the child's first "real" bed, a knapsack for the first day of school, moving to a new home, passing a driving test, a young driver's first car, adding an extra bedroom: All represent the movement to the next stage of life. Signifying to your customers that you have noticed, that you understand the importance of the event and share their joy, contributes to the enhancement of the purchase experience. Let me offer two examples, both involving furniture.

I recently asked the general manager of a large furniture retailer whether it sells children's beds, the kind that a two-year-old moves to when she becomes a "big girl" and sleeping in a crib is no longer appropriate. He said that his firm does indeed sell such beds, so I asked him to take me through the sales and delivery process. The bottom line is that this store treats such a sale as it does any other. The customer selects the product; it is delivered and set up if necessary.

Why would that retailer, if it truly appreciated the significance to the family of Sarah moving from crib to bed, not help celebrate the event? Why would the delivery team not bring along a helium-filled balloon with Sarah's name on it or some other "personalized" special gift to acknowledge the importance of the event? Now it's not simply the delivery of a new bed; it's a celebration of a major event in a young life. Won't her parents be impressed?

The second example involves a manufacturer of hand-built leather furniture. A typical suite of such furniture, which can run as much as $20,000, is bought by families who have reached a certain stage in life. When I asked the senior marketing executive of the company what, if anything, it did differently when it delivered the furniture, he seemed surprised by the question and was not sure what I was referring to. He did indicate that the company charged extra if they had to dismantle the furniture to get it through the door!

I reminded him that the customer may be paying $15,000 or more for this custom-made furniture and that it's likely a special occasion for the family. I then asked whether there was much scrap leather left over from the manufacture of sofas and chairs. Of course, there is. I then asked how much cost and effort would be involved if his skilled craftsmen were to make a set of leather bookmarks if the customer's new leather recliner is to be installed in a den or library, a set of leather coasters to protect teak coffee tables, or a leather doll for the five-year-old, or a leather "bone" for the dog—or all of these! The answer, of course, is that, in the context of a $15,000 sale, the cost and time involved would be minuscule.

Help customers celebrate, recognize the significance of what they have bought, show them you appreciate their business by adding a "nice touch" that sets you apart from competitors.

BAD EXPERIENCES: WHY DO THEY DO THAT?

We observed earlier that most customer experiences are quite ordinary, not at all memorable. Yet some companies have a knack for turning the ordinary into a bad experience. One has to wonder why some experiences occur when they obviously do not have to. For example, some employees seem to deliberately provoke customers. They say things that should never be said to customers. I was told recently of an encounter between a regular customer of the brand and an employee of a high-end fashion retailer. Having spent some time looking through the racks of not-inexpensive clothing, the customer found an item she wished to try on. She took it to an employee at the front of the store, who asked her size. When she was told the size the customer wished to try, the employee replied, "No, trust me, you will need the larger size." Adding further insult, the employee, noticing that the customer was wearing one of the firm's winter coats, commented, "That's one of ours, isn't it? I haven't seen that style for a long time. It's been quite a while since we carried that one." The customer walked out.

There is, I believe, a psychology at work in many customer experience situations that causes employees to do things, possibly unintentionally, that make the experience quite unpleasant. I changed hotels in Dublin several years ago because the senior porter at the hotel where I was staying refused to give me the key to my room one evening as I came back from a run. He argued that I had to produce identification before he could let me have my key; this despite the fact that I had been staying at the hotel regularly for three years and would not likely be carrying identification in my running shorts. I got the distinct impression that he was playing games with me, that he was having a fairly boring evening, and this was his way of livening up his day. I finally was able to get my key released by a front desk employee who recognized me, but I never went back, and over the next 10 years I stayed at a competing hotel probably 30 times.

STEPPING IN TO HELP WHEN BAD THINGS HAPPEN

Things do go wrong during customer interactions; or challenges and problems occur that have the potential to turn a positive experience into a negative one. Many such things arise in the normal course of events or are caused by factors that lie entirely outside your view and control—the customer herself, other customers, weather, heavy traffic, and so forth. In fact, much of the customer experience is often outside your control, but you have to be aware of what's happening so you can step in when you see things going off the rails.

You and your employees should develop a series of scenarios that address when things go wrong or at least anticipate events that can interfere with the customer's enjoyment of the experience. You need insight into situations that occur during typical customer interactions that have the potential to ruin the customer's day. What can go wrong and what are you going to do about it?

Many of the things that do go wrong are what we might term naturally occurring: people get hungry, kids act up, they need to find a toilet. To contribute to a positive experience in such situations means that you have to anticipate and provide solutions. The retail shopping experience can be enhanced by the availability of conveniently located, clean, family-friendly washrooms, by "adult" restaurants away from the food court where shoppers can enjoy a "nice" lunch, and by the provision of children's play areas where kids can blow off steam.

Tesco, the U.K. food retailer, as part of its ongoing search for customer insight conducted a survey of 3,000 parents and found that three-quarters of them thought that shopping with children is stressful, and more than half believed that kids have tantrums in supermarkets because they are bored. To contribute to a more positive experience for parents who dread shopping with their children, Tesco is developing, in collaboration with the cart manufacturer Wanzl, a Tantrum Tamer shopping cart that features an electronic screen for DVDs, CDs, and educational games.[7]

Endnotes

1. "Customer Experience: The Next Competitive Battleground," August 2004, www.insightexec.com/cgi-bin/library.cgi?action=detail&id=5072.
2. James Allen, Frederick F. Reichheld, and Barney Hamilton, "The Three 'Ds' of Customer Experience," *Harvard Business School Working Knowledge,* November 7, 2005. http://hbswk.hbs.edu/item.jhtml?id=5075&t=marketing
3. B. Joseph Pine II and James H. Gilmore, *The Experience Economy: Work Is Theatre & Every Business a Stage* (Boston: Harvard Business School Press, 1999).
4. David W. Norton, "Toward Meaningful Brand Experiences," *Design Management Journal* (Winter 2003): 19–25.
5. Kirthi Kalyanam and Monte Zweben, "The Perfect Message at the Perfect Moment," *Harvard Business Review* (November 2005): 112–120.
6. "Lloyds Call Centre Staff Scrap Scripts," January 13, 2006, www. insightexec.com/cgi-bin/item.cgi?id=131928.
7. "Trolley Treat in Store for Stroppy Kids," *The Guardian,* August 4, 2004.

6

THINGS YOU CAN MAKE POSSIBLE

We now move on to the highest level of the customer experience, where you create high levels of emotional value. To do this, a firm must address the ultimate level of the experience with the customer and look at the world differently, moving well beyond pleasant or entertaining experiences to create experiences that are personal and unique. We bring together here three of the most important concepts in the cultivation and enrichment of customer relationships: value, emotions, and experience.

ULTIMATE CUSTOMER EXPERIENCE

There are four approaches to the creation of a memorable experience for your customers, or at least four ways to consider how we might make the experience special. All involve a deeper look at the element of surprise and require an insightful view of the customer.

1. Customers are trying to accomplish something through the purchase of your products or services—remember the quarter-inch drill? They themselves may not even think past the purchase to what the purchase enables, and it is certain that many managers and executives fail to make that leap. But to get to the point where we are creating memorable experiences, we need to think about what we can make possible for the customer.

2. It is critically important that we understand how the customer defines success: What will it take for the customer to feel that she has achieved success, and what, in the business-to-business (B2B) context, will cause the customer's customers to notice something different, that they are being treated better?

3. It's important that we regularly consider how we can make customers look good in the eyes of those they need to impress. Everyone has someone in mind who is important and who is the object of your customer's attention: from dinner guests, to the boss, to grandchildren, to your customer's customers. If, through your interaction with customers, you can succeed in making them look good and feel proud, then you have created emotional value and earned their gratitude.

4. It's important to remember that there are many more important things happening in the lives of your customers than their purchase of your products. In fact, if you were to ask them what is *most* important to them, they would talk of their families, homes, vacations, pets, neighbors, a good book, golf, fishing, old movies, and a good bottle of wine. Your challenge is to help them to maintain closeness to these things and to enjoy them more easily and more often.

How do we make it possible for customers to experience things and achieve things they were not expecting to achieve, to succeed where they may not have expected to do so, to look good in the eyes of others who are important to them, and to more regularly participate in and enjoy the things that are most important in their lives? Understanding how to answer these questions requires that we delve more deeply into two central concepts that we have touched on earlier: customer expectations and the customer context.

EXPECTATIONS REVISITED

Customers come to any purchase situation with a set of expectations, and value is created for those customers to the extent that these expectations are met or exceeded. Let's review some of our discussion on customer expectations from Chapter 2 and add a couple of new points:

- Expectations contribute to customers' perception as to whether they have received quality, service, and value (all highly intangible and subjective concepts) in their dealings with a firm. Generally, where expectations are met, customers are satisfied.

- Expectations are based mainly on previous experiences with the firm and with others, and serve as reference points or standards against which the current experience may be compared.

- Expectations deal mainly with the level and quality of the products and service offered by the firm and not with innovative things that the firm may do. In other words, customer expectations relate principally to the components of the value proposition as conventionally defined.

- Expectations are bounded by context; customers perceive you as a company operating in a certain industry in a certain city. They expect you to do well the things that they expect firms in your industry and situation to do. They don't expect you to *behave* differently, and when you do, they are surprised.

- Many customer expectations are passive in that customers are unable to verbalize them. Such expectations will not rise to consciousness unless they are not met in some way or are greatly exceeded.

The idea of exceeding customer expectations appears to have captured the attention of a vast number of businesses today. We see evidence of it everywhere, as firms feel obliged to tell us in their advertising that they are committed to doing just that. But again, there is equally ample first-hand evidence that many firms regularly fail to meet even our most basic expectations and lose customers as a result. What is it about expectations that they do not seem to understand?

In my experience, many companies, when they talk of customer expectations, are really addressing those that are obvious and can be verbalized. If you are a florist, your customers likely expect you to have an acceptably wide selection of fresh flowers; to be good at floral arranging; to offer various services, such as delivery; to be open convenient hours; and to serve customers promptly and with courtesy. Believe me, if we were to ask a florist's customers what they expect, this is what they would typically answer. The generally acknowledged way to impress customers and to contribute to satisfaction is to exceed their expectations relating to quality or level of service. Meeting or even exceeding obvious, predictable expectations is relatively easy. Therefore, achieving customer satisfaction is likewise relatively easy.

I have referred to this as a *linear* exceeding of expectations because it involves linear thinking on the part of management: How can we do better what we already are expected to do? There's nothing wrong with the linear exceeding of expectations, except that all you will ever be is a pretty good florist. The fact that customer expectations are bounded, largely by the context in which a firm is operating, and extend mainly to the quality and level of service that the firm is expected to deliver, affords that firm an opportunity to contribute to the creation of emotional value by not only exceeding customer expectations relating to the functional aspects of product and service delivery but by actually doing things that are not expected of companies in that industry. We need more lateral thinking as to what we *could* do that customers are really not expecting. This will involve doing some new and different things.

DELIVERING THE UNEXPECTED

Tom Snyder, vice president of Huthwaite, Inc., an international sales performance improvement firm, recently identified situations where customers reported receiving extraordinary value from companies, to the extent that they were willing to pay a price premium, to redefine their relationship, to erect barriers to the seller's competitors, and to see the seller as a trusted advisor.[1] Sounds like an ideal situation to which firms should aspire; in fact, however, while many talk exactly that language, few really get there.

Snyder determined that successful selling organizations had:

- Revealed to their customers an unrecognized problem that the customers were experiencing
- Established for the buyers an unanticipated solution to problems that the buyers were experiencing
- Revealed unseen opportunities for the buyers' organizations

Snyder goes on to point out that the seller in all cases had succeeded in being seen by customers as more than a vendor of products and services, and instead served as a "broker of capabilities"—one who makes things possible, contributing to an expansion or redefinition of the customer's success.

What are the key words in Snyder's list? They include "unrecognized," "unanticipated," and "unseen." In other words, the customer did not see the solutions coming; they were unexpected. Snyder goes on to conclude that sellers must bring to the benefit of their customers insight that the customers are unable to achieve on their own. Simply put, customers don't know what they don't know. They don't realize that you may be able to do some different and valuable things for them.

The fact that the customer's expectations are bounded and extend mainly to the functional provision of products and services represents a genuine opportunity for your firm to step in with an unanticipated solution to a problem or the addition of value. You can create an impressive customer experience by noticing, by being thoughtful, and by personalizing. Think of situations where you might well say to your customers "Let us look after that for you"; "We thought you might be able to use a hand getting this done"; or "We'll be right over with that."

NEED FOR CONTEXTUAL INTELLIGENCE

Two different aspects of the role of context will help us better understand how we can create impressive experiences for customers. The first of these relates to the context in which the customer perceives the firm to be operating. The better you understand that context, the better position you will be in to create different and more meaningful customer experiences and to exceed expectations. Customer expectations are very much connected to the context in which the customer perceives the firm to operate. Customers expect your firm to behave in a certain way, because that's what companies in your industry do. It is when your firm does something that lies outside the context in which the customer has placed it that you have an opportunity to surprise the customer and to stand out.

But the customer is also operating within a context. The customer who is buying a product or service is doing so in order to accomplish some greater objective, to get something done, and to obtain a result. The product or service is a means to that end. The more you understand the customer's context and exactly what it is that the customer is setting out to accomplish, the greater your chances of doing things that will better allow the customer to achieve that goal, thereby becoming a participating partner.

Understanding the customer context will also better allow the firm to appreciate the nature of customer needs. A simplistic understanding of customer needs often extends only to the quality of the product or service and its provision. We often naively think that customers need quality products conveniently and readily available. But customers also need many other things that are potentially part of the broader context in which they are buying and using a particular product or service. The more a firm is able to address some of these wider-ranging customer needs, the broader will be its value proposition and the greater the likelihood of exceeding expectations.

Let's assume you are in the retail decorating business—you sell paint. On a Saturday morning, a customer comes into the store because she needs some paint to paint her dining room. But as we have observed before, she doesn't really *need* your paint; the paint is the vehicle that will allow her to accomplish other things, to address what might be termed *higher-order needs*. Clayton Christensen of the Harvard Business School, Scott Cook of Intuit, and Taddy Hall of the Advertising Research Foundation recently argued that the marketer's task is to understand the job that the customer wants to get done and then to design products and brands that fill that need. They maintain that every job that customers want to get done has a social, functional, and emotional dimension.[2]

Your customer is about to embark on an experience that will begin with the decision to paint the dining room and will end with that dinner party that she has planned for next Saturday evening. That's the broader context. You can play the role of supplier and provide her with paint, and possibly brushes, rollers, and tarps, or you can become her partner in obtaining accolades from her guests. Which do you want to be?

The more valuable role for you and the one that will deliver long-term payback to your firm is that of "partner." To get there, you have to engage in the gathering of contextual intelligence.[3] What else do you need to know, apart from the fact that the customer needs paint? The fact that she is painting a dining room may reveal certain other needs. She needs to ensure that the paint that she buys will match the furniture, carpet, and general decor of her home; will cover the paint that is currently on the walls; will dry quickly; and will have the appropriate finish. All of these concerns relate mainly to functional aspects of painting. But at the end of the day, what the customer really wants or needs is that the dining room will look "nice" and that she will be proud when her guests arrive for dinner next week—truly emotional needs.

So the customer's context and set of needs are much broader than getting paint on walls. Gerald Zaltman, in his book on how customers think, alleges that managers are often guilty of focusing on too narrow a view of their interaction with customers. He observed that "they focus 90 percent of their market research on the attributes and functional features of a product or service and their immediate psychological benefits, at the expense of their emotional benefits."[4]

I would further argue that companies are missing considerable opportunity to create customer delight by limiting their focus to the predictable functional aspects of the product. Customers don't need your paint; they need what your paint will make possible or, more correctly, what *you* can make possible. How can you inject your company into this situation so as to ensure that those accolades are forthcoming next Saturday night? You can be better equipped to play that role as a "broker of capabilities" if you know whether this is a new house, whether there is wallpaper on the dining room at the moment, whether the customer plans to do the painting herself or will hire a contractor, and so on. All of this, as well as your general knowledge of what's involved in painting a dining room, contributes to your contextual intelligence. The more you know about the context in which the customer is engaged, the more you can become part of the result that she is ultimately trying to achieve.

The solution you provide may range from recommending a particular color, type, or finish of paint, to providing a list of approved painting contractors, to offering in-store classes for first-time painters, to a full range of decorating services. The more you add, the more you exceed the customer's expectations, which may not have extended beyond buying paint. And you become much more than a paint store in her eyes.

B2B PERSPECTIVE

The same issue of looking past the obvious applies in the B2B context. Just as that customer needs more than paint, the B2B customer needs more than your office supplies, or equipment, or software. Just as she wants to impress family and friends and to feel good in her home, the B2B customer has higher-order needs as well. I am afraid that many companies selling to the B2B market lose sight of the fact that the customer has customers too. How often do you think of your customer's customers?

This is where it is extremely important to address the question of how the customer defines success, because your role in providing that B2B customer with products and services is principally related to contributing to his accomplishing something, to achieving success. But just as we need to know in some detail what is important to a paint customer and what she is really trying to accomplish, so too it is important to understand how B2B customers run their businesses and how they define success.

When I am working in the B2B space, I try to spend as much time as I can understanding my client's customers, what makes their day, what causes them great satisfaction, why they are in this business, and what keeps them awake at night. If I am successful in gaining such understanding, I can usually identify a number of ways that my client can build a stronger relationship with customers by doing some new and unexpected things and simply by behaving differently.

We often lose sight of the fact that our B2B customers are in business too. They have somewhat different goals and objectives from end consumers, but the creation of emotional value is no less important in this sector. Recently in a research project for a client, I asked a number of distributors of communications products how they define success in their businesses. Not surprisingly, a very large percentage of them spoke immediately of their own customers and how success only comes when *they* are satisfied. The question, then, for companies selling to B2B customers is how to make them look good in the eyes of their customers. How can we make them more successful in their dealings with their customers?

CREATE THAT ECLIPSE

We talked earlier in this chapter about the things that are important to your customers, that occupy a special place in their hearts and minds. These are the things to which your customers have a truly emotional attachment. Most of them are not commercial in nature but reflect personal dimensions of their lives. They are the people, possessions, events, and occasions that represent something special, that are an important part of what defines us as individuals. They would be truly missed if it were no longer possible for customers to experience them.

When I do customer interviews, I make it a point to find out as much as I can about the lives that customers lead, how they spend their time, what books they are reading, what movies they have enjoyed recently, what constitutes a perfect Saturday, where they love to go on vacation. These and many other insightful questions allow me to develop a much more complete picture not of customers but of people. Because, at the end of the day, they *are* people, after all, and your product or brand constitutes but a small part of their lives. But some brands occupy more space in the lives of their customers than others do, and it is possible for *you* and your brand to occupy a more substantial part.

Think of the concept of infiltration and how you might infiltrate the lives of your customers to a greater extent, how you can become more important to them. Think also about the concept of an eclipse and how your company or brand might gradually overlap an increasing portion of the lives of your customers.

Can you ever get to a total eclipse? I doubt it, but some brands have succeeded in occupying a very important place in the lives of their customers. I am thinking of such brands as Harley-Davidson and the fact that some of their strongest brand advocates not only wear the clothing, but have taken to such extreme measures as having the Harley logo tattooed on their bodies. Apple Macintosh users are similarly attached to that brand, as are the fans of various professional sports teams. To create the eclipse, your company may have to provide opportunities for customers to gather to share their passion for some activity or to engage in that activity more easily or on a more regular basis. For example, in a project for a shopping center, we found that the target group of fashion-conscious women were most interested in and preoccupied with their families, homes, and careers, but close to the top of their lists of things that they enjoyed doing or experiencing were reading and wine. This led to a strategy of getting closer to these customers and of playing a more important role in their lives by arranging readings in the mall by well-known authors, the establishment of a series of book clubs, and the holding of monthly wine-tasting evenings—all of this despite the fact that there was no bookstore or wine store in the mall.

Once we knew the interests of the target customer group, a *predictable* marketing- or sales-oriented response would have been to try to attract a wine store and bookstore to the mall as tenants. While this very likely would have been a good idea, the approach that we recommended goes much further in meeting the shopping center's goal of playing a more important role in the lives of their customers, of being more to them than just a shopping mall.

A second approach to the eclipse strategy involves the more traditional route of sponsorship. By identifying things in which target customers are interested, a company can more easily develop a sponsorship or association strategy that is based on the notion of "fit." For sponsorships to be effective in building an emotional bond with customers, there must be a clear, strategic connection between the sponsoring brand, the interests of its target customer groups, and the event or property being sponsored. Where that fit exists, the message is clearly sent to the customer that this brand is interested in the same things that she's interested in. Where the fit is less obvious, customers likely will wonder why the company is involved in such a thing.

If your customers are passionate about gardening, you might want to sponsor the local garden show. If they are into snowboarding, sponsoring competitions at the local ski hill makes more sense. A note of caution: Don't sponsor the garden show simply because *you* are passionate about gardening; your customers may not be.

TWO BOXES, ACTUALLY...

How often have you heard the criticism that managers and executives, possibly even at your company, are guilty of "thinking inside the box"? In many companies with which I have been associated in recent years, managers stand guilty as charged. They do indeed regularly think inside that box, and, even more important, they behave inside the box as well. They regularly think and behave like people who make and sell things, not as people who make things happen.

When you ask many managers how they might improve the performance of their company, many will immediately put on their sales hats and try to identify ways to increase current sales levels. If you look for ideas concerning how they might improve interaction with their customers, many will respond with examples of how they could do certain things better. The problem is that much of what I typically hear represents linear thinking; they tend to suggest how they might improve on what they already do. Such thinking is not especially creative and usually does not involve the firm getting outside the box in which its managers have placed it. Such an approach to customers does little to allow the firm to really stand out from the competition.

These executives are also usually guilty of not wearing their customer hats to work, of not seeing past what they make and what they do to what they can make possible for customers and what they can do to make things easier for them. Recall our reference to the customer hat in Chapter 1 and my observation that many managers are critical of other companies with which they deal as customers but seemingly unable to identify with their own customers who are expressing the same degree of emotional disconnect. Although they themselves are experienced and seasoned customers, they seem unable to see their own companies from the customer perspective.

If you are going to be able to create meaningful experiences for your customers, then you have to be able to both think and behave outside the box. To do this, you must first understand why this boxed thinking is happening in the first place. But before we address that issue, let me suggest that we have a very important second box to open, one that represents an opportunity rather than a problem.

If you talk at length with enough customers in enough research projects, eventually you will come to the conclusion that customers are not particularly creative when it comes to suggesting how a company might impress them. They think inside their own box. When asked how a firm may exceed their expectations, customers tend to respond with suggestions that pertain to doing the predictable things unpredictably well, to the *linear* exceeding of expectations. Thus, they say that they would be impressed and highly satisfied if the firm would deliver more quickly, have items in stock, have lots of checkouts open, and do it all on time and with no errors or mistakes. And, by the way, they'd like it if prices were lower as well. These expectations extend mainly to the predictable things that customers expect companies to provide. Thus, your customers are not going to be particularly helpful when it comes to identifying ways that you can surprise them and contribute to that elusive emotional connection. As Henry Ford is alleged to have sagely observed, "If I had asked people what they wanted, they would have said faster horses."

The fact that your customers also have their own box inside which they tend to think provides you with an important opportunity. You can strive to achieve higher levels of customer satisfaction by continually improving the things that you do, thereby achieving some marginal degree of success, as long as you do them better than the competition. Or you can surprise customers by doing things that they do not expect you to do, by behaving outside the box that you and your customers both have you in.

WHAT WILL IT TAKE?

You can generally satisfy your customers and probably become known as a pretty good company in your market or industry simply by doing really well the things that customers expect you to do, through the linear exceeding of their predictable expectations, by delivering the kind and level of service that they would like to receive. Customer delight, however, is more likely to occur when you exceed mainly subconscious expectations in a lateral way, by addressing needs that customers typically would not associate with a firm such as yours, by delivering components of the value proposition that they do not expect. Thus, surprise plays a central role in the creation of meaningful customer experiences.

What is it going to take to change companies into truly customer-focused organizations that are committed to creating surprising, high-level experiences for their customers? In my view, the ability of a company to create such experiences lies entirely with the managers of that firm and in the culture they have created and the people they employ. Here are some tips:

- Figure out how to get more creativity into the organization and its people.
- Avoid the temptation to look for short-term financial payback in every initiative taken with respect to the customer. We have to somehow resist the pressures to look for an immediate sales effect.
- Allow (and even encourage) employees to bend and even break the rules from time to time.
- Hire more employees whose personalities are characterized by high levels of empathy, sensitivity, and curiosity.
- Encourage more lateral thinking—what else could we be doing?
- Instill a culture that encourages employees to be constantly looking for opportunities to impress.

LET'S GET CREATIVE

An examination of the role of creativity is important to an understanding of how companies can create emotional value for their customers. As we have observed, both customers and managers tend to think inside the box when it comes to value creation. Even when managers and customers think creatively, this creativity appears bounded in that both groups tend to focus on such things as product innovation or new uses for an existing product or improved performance at the things the firm already does. Psychological research on creativity may help us understand why this is so. It may also help identify techniques that we can use to create unique value for customers by addressing needs that they would not normally expect a company like yours to address.

Creativity has been a largely underresearched area, but psychologists have recently begun to pay more attention to the subject. The two key elements that are present in many definitions of creativity are *novelty* and *utility*. An idea that no one has thought of before would not be considered creative if it had no practical value. Conversely, a practical idea is not creative unless it is in some way original. If we are to be more creative in the identification of ways to impress customers, we must come up with ideas that not only have not been tried before, but also that are useful to the customer; in short, they must add value in the customer's eyes.

An idea need not be a major breakthrough to be considered creative. Some of the best innovations are simple changes in a process or design that can make the customer's life much easier. Once a novel idea is created, it may appear so logical that it is difficult to believe that it came about from a creative rather than a logical process. A firm that can come up with a better experience (that is unique and useful) for customers that appears obvious to customers once it is put in place demonstrates creativity, because customers had not thought of it and are surprised that the firm has. The problem is that humans have a tendency to think in structured and predictable ways that prevent them from using their capacity for creativity.

Cognitive psychologists have explained this tendency toward bounded thinking in different ways. Several refer to the tendency of people to be trapped by prior experiences, a phenomenon often termed structured imagination and defined as "the fact that when people use their imagination to develop new ideas, those ideas are heavily structured in predictable ways by the properties of existing categories and concepts."[5] There is a general tendency for new ideas to preserve many of the central properties of existing concepts, and this tendency can act as a constraint on creativity.

Bounded thinking is seen in customers who will, as we regularly observe in qualitative research, define their needs in rather narrow, functional terms. Their verbalized expectations tend to be predictable. This "inside-the-box thinking" may be explained in part by the phenomenon of structured imagination, which would lead customers to draw on existing concepts. For instance, a customer who is asked what it would take for him to be impressed with a moving company might answer that he would like the company to arrive and deliver on time, pack and unpack things carefully, ensure (ideally) no breakage, keep the family informed of anticipated delivery date, and generally be easy to deal with, respond to calls, and be available when needed. In short, his expectations would not likely extend beyond the core components of a moving company's value proposition.

This lack of customer creativity represents a tremendous opportunity for firms to be creative on behalf of the customer. That is, if firms and their employees can put themselves in the customer's place and identify novel ways to improve the customer's experience—ways that the customer had not thought of—the customer will be surprised and impressed. But why don't firms appear to be terribly creative when it comes to creating experiences for their customers? Part of the answer appears to lie in organizational culture. Not only are some organizations unable to foster creativity; as we discuss in Chapter 9, some may actually be constraining it.

REALLY THINKING OUTSIDE THE BOX

Funeral services represent a great example of how the kind of thinking presented in this chapter can be applied. The people who work in this industry represent the ultimate in caring and sensitivity. They have to. This is one of a small number of service industries that I describe as "can't fail"; others include wedding photography and surgery. All are involved in highly emotive situations, and much depends on their carrying out their roles with no mistakes. These represent situations from which it is virtually impossible to recover if mistakes are made.

The funeral industry has been around literally forever but has not been characterized by high levels of innovation or creativity. Of course, there has been some change as funeral directors moved to offer cremation services as well as the more conventional interment. In an effort to remain competitive in a highly competitive industry, many firms now also offer prearranged and prepaid funerals, which not only serve to reduce the confusion and trauma typically associated with the death of a loved one, but also provide the funeral director with cash flow and a guaranteed sale at the time of death.

But to go back to our new view of the world, cremations and prearranged funerals are simply variations on the services that funeral homes have traditionally delivered. The question is, what else could funeral homes be good at? Their area of expertise extends to what? The answer may lie in the fact that funeral homes typically and most often deal with the deaths of elderly people. Most often they are dealing with the families of people who have lived a long life, the last few years of which have brought certain health and other challenges for the deceased and for members of the immediate family. Rather than simply selling a prearranged funeral, as valuable as that service is in providing peace of mind, why would a funeral home not try to extend its involvement with the family to provide much-needed and unanticipated services relating to the latter stages of life?

With large numbers of people living well into their 80s and 90s, many decisions have to be made by the elderly and by their families. Provision of health and nursing care, insurance, preparation of wills, estate and other forms of financial planning, admission to nursing homes are all decisions that must be faced by increasing numbers of families. Typically, most families are ill-prepared to make such decisions, particularly as they are often made in very emotional circumstances. What's needed is a professional approach from someone who is knowledgeable about legal and other matters, knows his or her way around various social agencies and regulations, and can lend a sympathetic ear and provide sound advice.

Funeral homes are well positioned to take on such a role, as they are already seen to be empathetic, caring, and professional, and they already have an appreciation for what families go through as a loved one gets older. Most families have no idea what to expect and literally don't know where to turn. Funeral homes can become more than the caring people to whom we turn at the time of death. They can become experts in late-life planning.

GREAT CLEANERS? NOT ANYMORE...

A similar opportunity arises when the product or service you provide becomes increasingly commoditized. This is the case when customers see no real difference between what you offer and what is offered by your competitors. The inevitable result of such a situation is that customers gravitate toward price as the differentiator. Suddenly you find yourself competing on price, and we all know what a slippery slope that represents. The challenge is to differentiate, and it's not easy. How do you give a customer a reason to come to you first in a nondifferentiated industry, and to pay a higher price for your services?

Several years ago, I was introduced to the managing director of a company in the United Kingdom that specialized in cleaning commercial properties. It had been in business for many years and had been successful in capturing a large share of the commercial cleaning business. Every night it had teams of employees cleaning office buildings, airports, hospitals, motorway restaurants, and other buildings up and down the UK. The problem was, as the managing director explained to me, that the industry had become very competitive and highly automated in recent years. Building owners and property managers had capitalized on the increased level of competition and had begun calling for tenders for cleaning services and awarding contracts on the basis of the lowest cost per square foot.

The managing director indicated that his margins were being squeezed as prices came down; he was unable to pay higher wages and was having difficulty retaining staff. He was frustrated by his inability to convince his customers that his company could clean better than the competitors who were underbidding him. When I asked him whether his firm could clean floors, terrazzo, walls, carpets, draperies, window blinds, marble, counter-tops, and other building components, the answer was, in all cases, "Yes." When I asked if his company could clean to the exacting standards of hygiene required in places where food is served, in operating rooms, and lab-oratories, the answer was again "Yes."

I then asked if he could accurately determine the cost to clean various surfaces. Again, "Yes." "So," I went on, "if I were to ask you to tell me the best surfaces to put into a new building or when renovating so as to optimize the cost of cleaning over the lifetime of the building and to achieve certain standards of hygiene and cleanliness, could you do it?" His answer was, predictably "Yes."

I told him that I didn't think his was a great cleaning company at all; they were experts in surfaces. Suddenly a repositioning seemed appropri-ate. The problem was that he had never looked at his company as anything other than a great cleaning company. With this new perspective, he could differentiate his firm from competitors, who had convinced customers that they could clean as well as he could, and take his company in a different direction, elevating cleaning to a different level and providing an unex-pected service and new forms of value to clients.

INTEL FACTOR

The B2B world affords many opportunities to create emotional value for customers because of the fact that every one of a firm's B2B clients has cus-tomers of its own. As observed earlier, it is surprising how often managers appear to ignore this fact. The reason a business needs to buy various prod-ucts and services is to enhance its ability to serve its own customers, to be more successful. I have worked with a number of businesses that had devel-oped innovative products or services and were having difficulty convincing prospective customers to adopt them, since in many cases it would mean dislodging an existing competitor that had the business.

I was working with the publisher of tax preparation software a few years ago. The firm was facing a considerable challenge making inroads against the market leader in selling to independent tax accountants, lawyers, and consultants. We developed an approach that saw us advertising to the small businesses that are the clients of such professionals, with the message that they should look for a tax preparer who uses this brand of software. Essentially, the message became "You can't be sure it's right, unless your accountant is using this software." The plan called for providing tax professionals with links for their Web sites and decals for their doors that labeled them a "Brand _____ Approved Tax Preparer." Just as there are customers who would not buy a laptop that doesn't have the "Intel Inside" logo on it, we wanted to encourage end customers to insist that their tax preparer is using our brand of software.

While the sales staff of the software company was calling on its prospective clients, selling the product on its technical merits, ease of use, and current updates that reflected the most recent changes in tax law and regulations, we found that the customers' customers were mainly interested in having their taxes prepared accurately. They needed to be assured that their tax returns would be prepared correctly so that they would pay the correct amount of tax and not a penny more. Our pull approach to marketing focused on promoting to the end customer to encourage them to go looking for tax professionals who used this brand of software and to be reassured when their tax preparer displays the logo on the office door. For their part, customers of the software company were impressed by the new direction and were quite prepared to feature the software brand in their own marketing efforts.

SUDDENLY IT'S A DIFFERENT VALUE PROPOSITION

Think about your business in a different way, get past what you have been doing for years, and redefine what you offer customers. It is about an experience, not a product. That customer interaction is a situation that will, in a holistic sense, contribute to the accomplishment of something of value to the customer. How can you inject your company into that experience in such a way that you will be seen to have contributed to the successful outcome?

This kind of thinking requires that you view your value proposition in a much broader sense. It no longer consists of what you sell, make, or do, but must be more broadly viewed to also include what you could do to contribute to achieving results for customers. It's about what you make possible and can do for them. If you start to think this way, you are forced to change your value proposition and your positioning. You are not what you thought you were or what customers thought you were; you are much more than that.

The innovative thinking to get you to this new state does not have to represent a dramatic departure from your current operation. By adding some new and different things, you suddenly transform your business from a place where customers can buy things to a place where they may actually enjoy the experience and obtain far more than they had bargained for. This response is seen, for example, among families who shop at IKEA stores worldwide.

One of the features of IKEA that families find most attractive is the supervised child care in stores; parents can leave their children in a trusted environment while they shop. It is unusual to find a retailer that provides such a facility; as a result, it is unexpected and more valued.

You see, IKEA's value proposition isn't just about quality, self-assembled furniture that represents great value for money. It *is* about these things, but it's much more. It's also about the sense of accomplishment that results from the customer's involvement in the assembly of the furniture. It's also about the play areas and restaurants in IKEA stores that make shopping there much more tolerable. I was leading a workshop several years ago in Malmö, Sweden, with a group of senior IKEA marketing managers who often referred to the fact that they were focused on their "best customers." When I finally asked them who they considered their best customers to be, they replied, "Our best customers are those who like us the most."

STEPPING BACK

There exists the opportunity in virtually every business to elevate the customer experience to a new level, if only we can be creative about how we approach it. We have to understand and appreciate that we often have the company and its customers operating as two separate entities, functioning in two different contexts, and thinking inside two separate boxes. The challenge is to gain greater overlap with the lives of customers by understanding their view of the context and by capitalizing on the many opportunities that present themselves every day to surprise and impress customers by behaving outside your box.

To raise your company to the level where customers are going to be impressed and emotional connections are being built demands a different way of thinking about customers. As the examples presented in this chapter suggest, you need to think past the sale to uncover problems that customers may not even know they have, to put forth solutions to problems that they certainly don't expect you to address, and to identify opportunities for them to be more successful than they had anticipated. To do so means that you must achieve the kind of customer insight that will allow you to spot such opportunities and then foster a creative culture that will allow employees to identify and implement solutions

Endnotes

1. Tom Snyder, "Escaping the Price-Driven Sale: Selling to Clients at a Premium," Huthwaite, Inc., 2005, www.huthwaite.com.

2. Clayton M. Christensen, Scott Cook, and Taddy Hall, "Marketing Malpractice: The Cause and the Cure," *Harvard Business Review* (December 2005): 74–83.

3. *See* Arch G. Woodside, *Market-Driven Thinking: Achieving Contextual Intelligence* (Burlington, MA, Butterworth Heinemann, 2005); and Robert J. Sternberg, "Culture and Intelligence," *American Psychologist* 59, no. 5 (July–August 2004): 325–338.

4. Gerald Zaltman, *How Customers Think: Essential Insights into the Mind of the Market* (Boston: Harvard Business School Press, 2003), p. 18.

5. Thomas B. Ward, "What's Old About New Ideas?" in *The Creative Cognition Approach,* ed. Steven M. Smith, Thomas B. Ward, and Ronald A. Finke (Cambridge, MA: MIT Press, 1995), p. 157.

7

PAYBACK TIME

The message in this chapter is simple: Companies that develop a customer strategy that leads to genuine customer relationships can realize tremendous payback. It is also a fact, however, that the measurement of that payback is a difficult if not impossible task for most firms, akin to trying to obtain an accurate measure of the effectiveness of advertising—a task that has been frustrating advertisers for years—or of calculating a precise return on a company's investment in employee training.

Some companies have developed certain measures in an attempt to capture evidence of the results of a more customer-focused approach to their business. We will discuss some of those measurement tools when we turn our attention to the subject of metrics in the next chapter. But if you are looking for solid evidence of short-term, monetary payback from building more solid customer relationships, you may be deluding yourself.

Many firms are far too focused on producing a numbers-based measure of the return on the investment in their customer relationship *program*. It is precisely that view of the world that actually contributes to the dilemma: companies viewing customer relationship building as a *program* or a *project*. Customer relationship management (CRM) Web sites and publications are full of articles that attempt to deal with the issue of return on investment (ROI) on CRM; virtually all of them address the question of the ROI in CRM technology and software.

I'd like to step back from this focus on ROI and address the fundamental question of whether a company's initiative to develop stronger customer relationships will, over time, make any difference to sales and the bottom line. I am, of course, convinced that it will. But we may not be able to quantify the payback to the satisfaction of those who are looking for measurable, short-term financial evidence.

It is a fact of business life that some outcomes and indicators of success are very difficult to quantify. Others are virtually impossible to quantify, particularly in small and medium-size businesses where typically we are unable to track sales and profitability by customer and where we simply can't get a good handle on outcomes such as customer churn, cost to serve, and word of mouth. Few firms, including the biggest, have such data at their fingertips or in customer databases. In the absence of such information, the danger is that important decisions will be made on the basis of data that are suspect and actually do not relate to what should be considered the real payback from relationship building. An even more important danger is that some companies will not proceed toward greater customer centricity and the building of stronger customer relationships *precisely because* they are unable to measure outcomes to their satisfaction.

The bottom line is that you can't measure everything that you would like to measure with the degree of accuracy that you would like to have. Some important things are impossible to quantify, even for very large companies with big research budgets and even bigger computers.

But perhaps we don't have to quantify everything. I realize that executives like to have numbers to justify investments, but some things simply make intuitive sense. Based on your own experience and evidence from your own customers, isn't it obvious that customers will go back again and give more of their business to firms where they are treated well and made to feel good?

Okay, you still need some more evidence to convince the folks in the executive offices to free up the budget to get the customer relationship job done. We'll talk about the principles that underlie the payback argument in this chapter, and we'll provide some metrics you can use in Chapter 8.

CUSTOMER RELATIONSHIPS AS ASSETS

What is the value of a solid customer relationship? More and more firms are asking questions such as this as they attempt to measure nonfinancial or intangible assets and attribute economic value to them. This is happening at a time when intellectual capital, brands, human resources, and training are more important to some companies than the value of their plant and equipment.

More than financial measures are needed to gain a better understanding of the true value of the future potential of a company. In this context, a traditional accounting approach is inadequate because it fails to take into account the kinds of measures that are of critical importance to those who are focused on the long-term value of the firm's customer relationships. It is the customer who is responsible for the company's future earnings. It is essential, therefore, that the company place a value on the long-term stream of earnings that results from genuine customer relationships.

Therefore, customer relationships represent just as important a financial asset as any of the physical assets that a firm may own, and they rank right up there with the value of a loyal and well-trained employee group and the value of the company's brand, both of which are assets that are today generally acknowledged to contribute to the company's long-term worth. Customer relationships should be managed strategically, just as any other major assets of a firm.

CURSE OF CUSTOMER CHURN

Acquiring new customers is costly. If customers stay with your business only for a short time or if they buy once and never come back, you do not recover these costs and you must spend more to recruit new customers. This is the curse of customer "churn" to which many businesses are exposed. This revolving-door phenomenon is endemic in highly competitive industries where there is little product differentiation and competition is based largely on price. In these situations, customer turnover and short-term customer attraction is encouraged through cutthroat price competition. A certain segment of customers—the switchers—do very well for themselves by constantly switching companies to take advantage of the best price incentives.

A major problem in some companies that do not have good customer records and databases is that it is extremely difficult to identify customers who are leaving. Customer churn is invisible to firms that don't have the ability to track customers. Unless companies have data, they may not even realize that they've lost customers. Since many customers are anonymous, they can leave without being noticed. In any case, the challenge is to give customers a reason to stay, which means having to overcome the attraction of price incentives by adding a form of value that transcends price appeal.

Many firms view customer churn as a short-term issue. They throw money at it, using promotions and deals to keep their customers. These short-term solutions will not retain customers in the long run. It will simply keep the switchers hanging on a little longer. A long-term customer strategy that focuses on building loyal customers is much more sustainable because several factors contribute to a loyal customer's profit-making potential over time.

Going back 15 years or more, authors like Frederick Reichheld and Earl Sasser demonstrated the payback to be realized from the reduction of customer turnover.[1] They showed that a 5 percent increase in customer loyalty can double a firm's profitability. Most companies now generally accept that customer retention is a good thing. When customers defect to the competition, they take their profit-making potential with them. If a company could see the real cost of losing a customer, it would be more likely to make investments in time and people to retain as many customers as possible.

WHAT IS A LOYAL CUSTOMER WORTH?

Those who write about the calculation of customer lifetime value (CLV) are often making certain assumptions about the availability of data. The fact is that the vast majority of firms do not have the necessary data available to make such calculations. The temptation, and the avowed intention in many firms, is to attempt to calculate some measure of customer value and then to create a categorization of customers ranging from very valuable to not at all valuable. This categorization is then used to tailor marketing and customer contact activity directed toward the "value segments." Many nascent relationships are nipped in the bud as companies take preemptory action to terminate customers who are deemed to be unprofitable.

In the absence of accurate data on the *real* value of a customer (and few firms have the necessary information), firms often default to whatever data are available; usually these are terribly simplistic indicators of customer value, most notably historic spend data or (where available) profits. Let's not confuse value with profitability. The former is long term and future oriented; the latter much more short term and historic. The long-term value of a customer means exactly that—the value that this customer will bring to your firm if you can keep him coming back for a long time into the future.

Why then do firms estimate future value using historic sales data? The answer is that this is the only information they have, and they are often under pressure to come up with estimates of customer value. CLV is seen very simplistically as the net present value of future profits. Much has been written on activity-based costing and customer profitability analysis, all of which assumes, of course, the availability of customer data. The truth is that many (likely most) firms simply don't have detailed customer data and have not cracked the nut of how to allocate costs accurately to individual customers. If firms don't have the data, often they make dangerous assumptions and develop decision rules so that they *can* come up with some measure of customer profitability.

Focusing on historic and current sales, or even on future revenue projections, does not provide a sufficient measure of true customer value. If we really want to know what a customer is worth to us, in strictly monetary terms that can be related to current profitability, then we need to know something about what it is costing us to serve that customer. Only those companies with sophisticated information systems that can capture data about customer purchases and can calculate and attribute costs are in a position even to get close to an estimate of customer contribution to profits. Customer profitability analysis and similar approaches are geared toward large firms with sophisticated information systems.

Customer profitability estimates, where they are calculated, are typically linked to directly allocated revenues and costs. As a result, estimates of CLV miss a lot of softer, difficult-to-measure factors. Even if we can allocate costs to customers (which would involve the establishment of overhead allocation rules and a system for recording inputs, both of which are fraught with implementation problems), such systems simply cannot capture other things, such as referrals and the customer's ability to influence business.

Loyal customers who have established relationships with a firm bring that company far more than the direct monetary benefits that are generally accounted for in the form of sales revenues. The sales to loyal customers represent merely the tip of the benefits iceberg. Small firms that really know their customers well—that is, they know much more about them than what they buy and how often they use their frequent-shopper card—are in a position to appreciate the ability of loyal customers to influence other business.

REAL ROI FROM CUSTOMER RELATIONSHIPS

The real return on your investment in building customer relationships is difficult to calculate. As with many concepts that we have examined in this book, there are hard (monetary) and soft (nonmonetary) components to the ROI. As reflected in Exhibit 7.1, the hard side is related to financial numbers and is more easily captured and calculated in those firms where data are available. We can see sales and profitability change over time. But we can't generally observe changes in nonmonetary factors such as referrals, comfort level, and reduced price sensitivity.

Let's give some thought to the eight factors that together contribute to the real value that your firm will experience if you build solid, long-lasting relationships with your customers:

1. **The future value of the stream of earnings.** This is the most obvious component of the ROI, and it is easy to project based on historic data, with assumptions that repeat business will continue at the present

Exhibit 7.1   Return on Customer Relationships

Monetary Components	Nonmonetary Components
• Future stream of earnings • Growth in share of wallet • Lower cost to serve • Lower price consciousness	• Increased comfort level • Increased referrals • Influence on other business • Tendency to forgive mistakes

rate. Clearly, if customers continue to buy from you, and do so well into the future, you will reap the rewards. Even if you don't have actual data by customer, you can calculate a reasonable estimate of what a loyal customer will deliver directly over a 10- or 15-year period.

2. **They will spend more.** Customers tend to spend more money with a business the longer they deal with it. This is the so-called share of wallet effect. As they get more comfortable dealing with you, they will give you more of their business. In insurance, for example, over time more and more customers consolidate their home and auto business with a single provider.

3. **They will cost less to serve.** New customers are costly to attract; loyal ones cost much less to keep. Employees spend time getting to know new customers and recovering from mistakes because they are not familiar with their needs. Loyal customers, however, are already established, and employees are familiar with them so that they are easier to serve. Reichheld and Sasser documented more than 15 years ago that customer profitability is likely to increase over time as account service costs decline.[2]

4. **They are less price sensitive.** Loyal customers are much less likely to quibble over price and may even reach the stage in their relationship where they *may not even ask the price.* This is evidence that customers place more *value* on other things. In many situations where genuine relationships exist, the price being charged for the product or service may be among the least important determinants of customer satisfaction. Bruce Hunter, former vice president of Marketing at Kraft Foods, once observed that having very strong customer relationships allowed Kraft to sell-through a higher percentage of inventory at full price.

5. **They get comfortable.** When genuinely loyal customers are asked why they go back to a company over and over again, they often refer to the fact that they feel "comfortable" dealing with the firm. They have come to know the staff, and there is a sense of routine and even habit. They have no incentive to leave. They have developed a feeling of trust that comes with familiarity and will go back because "they know me there."

6. **They spread positive word of mouth.** Loyal customers become ambassadors for the company, or what some refer to as "part-time marketers." Referrals from friends and family are powerful endorsements for a company's products and services, and are often given greater credibility than paid communications. As loyal customers refer others to a business, the business realizes new earnings potential and opportunities to build even more customer relationships. Frederick Reichheld feels so strongly about the power of referrals that he suggests that this is the only piece of information companies need to know to assess the strength of customer relationships.[3]

7. **They influence other business.** Consciously or subconsciously, loyal customers serve as passive ambassadors for your firm and brand. When they are seen using your product, or eating at your restaurant, or driving your car, they are sending a message that they implicitly endorse the brand. This serves as an informal influence on other customers, a form of personal product placement.

8. **They are more forgiving.** The relationship that has been built with genuinely loyal customers represents an insurance policy for the firm. It's like money in the bank when things do go wrong. Genuinely loyal customers are more likely to give a firm a second chance or to overlook mistakes, within reason. The typical response is "Don't worry about it; these things happen."

VI³C: SOME JUST LOOK GOOD ON YOU

There are some customers out there that you probably should have on your customer or client list, even though they may not currently be profitable in their own right. These are what might be labeled strategically important customers. They are the folks you would rather not see flying on the competitor's airline, or carrying a competing cell phone, or buying their furniture from the guy down the street. Even though you may not make a lot of money on them, it would look good if you could count them among your customers.

Several years ago, I developed for a client the concept of the VI^{3}C—the Very I I I Customer (Important, Influential, and Interesting). We developed a strategy that identified those members of the target segment who would be considered important, influential, and interesting. These customers were then placed in a specific VI^{3}C subsegment that was singled out for particular attention and for relationship building. The main point is that these were individuals whom we wanted to see carrying and using our products, not because they necessarily buy a lot, but because of the business they have the potential to influence and simply because it would enhance our brand to be associated with them.

In a fairly small market or in situations where the list of potential customers is not especially long, preparing a list of those customers who should be on the VI^{3}C list is a surprisingly easy process. In the case of my telecommunications client, we were able, over the course of a month or so, to prepare a list of 200 individuals to be placed in the VI^{3}C category. Many were already customers, and the strategy to be followed in their case was to retain and grow their business—to strengthen the relationship. More difficult was the identification of target VI^{3}C customers whom we wished to attract as customers.

If you adopt the VI^{3}C approach, you should define the "important" qualifier as identifying customers who are already spending a lot with you, who are "up and comers," or who are on the leading edge in their field. They are prominent in the community, often quoted or sought out for opinion. They are important not only in terms of what they buy or might buy, but also because of the leadership positions they occupy.

"Influential" people are those who have the potential to affect the opinions and decisions of other prospective customers. They have business, family, and social connections that may be obvious, but may also be hidden from public view. In the latter case, you may have to do some digging around to identify those connections. You need to know not only what boards they sit on, but also with whom they associate and who listens to them. The fact that a person has been the regular tennis partner of a business leader for many years may be a very important piece of information.

Finally, the "interesting" label is often the most exciting to work on. What you are looking for are those prospective customers who are doing exciting and noteworthy things. They may not be accounting for much business at the moment, but they are newsworthy or in the public eye. They may be volunteer leaders, inventors, sports celebrities, award winners, and others who find themselves in the limelight. These are people whom others look up to and with whom it is simply good to be associated. Their public prominence rubs off on your brand.

Developing a strategy to target a VI^3C segment will involve some work on your part, both in developing the list itself and also in profiling each individual on that list. The profiling exercise is important because you will need to customize the approach to these customers, and the more you know about them the better.

A CUSTOMER'S SPHERE OF INFLUENCE

Often a business doesn't realize exactly whom it is impressing or offending or what volume of business it is placing at risk. The concept of sphere of influence or association is at work here. Customers will leave a business or will terminate a relationship for reasons that have absolutely nothing to do with marketing as we have known it. They may leave for reasons that have nothing to do with them personally but rather because of how a friend, family member, or associate was treated. This ripple effect cannot be ignored. Developing a close, genuine relationship with customers is, once again, something of an insurance policy. It protects not only the business that flows from that customer directly but also the business that she may influence by association.

Certain aspects of the value of the loyal customer are difficult to observe and measure, but may in fact be contributors to long-term customer value: the related concepts of word of mouth and sphere of influence. Customers who have a solid, mutually beneficial relationship with a company, where they are treated well and made to feel important and valued, will delight in telling their friends, family, and associates. They will become advocates for the company and bring in untold volumes of business.

Simon Cooper, now President of Ritz-Carlton, in his former role as CEO of Delta Hotels, would motivate his employees to provide exceptional service to their guests by telling them that every business guest at a Delta Hotel has a potential lifetime value of $300,000. Even the most road-weary business traveler would take many years to rack up this volume of business in room charges alone. But factor in the possibility that the customer concerned may influence the travel policy for his company or is a member of the board of directors of a professional organization that has to decide where to hold its annual convention, and it is easy to see how one guest has the potential to influence much more than $300,000 in total future sales. This illustrates the dual concepts of referral business and sphere of influence. Yet few companies make any attempt to measure the extent to which their customers are prepared to engage in such referral behavior. Large volumes of potential revenue are at stake if you upset them, but you'll never know you lost it!

WHAT WE STAND TO LOSE WHEN THEY LEAVE

Many companies today are paying a lot more attention to customer churn, acknowledging that they can't afford to be losing business as a result of regular customers leaving to take their business elsewhere. Many of these firms have developed models to estimate the value of the business they are losing when a customer leaves. Let me suggest that in many cases, they are merely scratching the surface; whatever their estimate of the value of a lost customer, it is probably at least three or four times that level.

A simple, financially focused view would lead us to conclude that we lose that customer's stream of business. Take the average annual revenue from that customer, multiply it by an estimate of the future active life of the customer, and discount it by some appropriate discount rate, and we have the net present value of that customer's business. If we are really sophisticated, we can even compute profitability estimates. But we are not taking into account the amount of business that the departing customer may be able to influence.

Allow me to share a personal experience with you that I believe illustrates this principle rather well. Several years ago my wife and I ended our "relationship" with a major bank with which we had been dealing for more than 30 years. Although we had not been particularly impressed with the attention we were paid by the bank, we had given them all of our banking business, as had our three daughters, all of whom had by then graduated from university and were employed in professional positions with major organizations. The bank had all of our family's business.

Our relationship with the bank was not a negative one. We heard from them rarely and then usually to try to sell us some investment product. Nevertheless, we were not provoked to change the situation until two events happened within a few weeks of each other. On the first occasion, a fairly senior employee of the bank made a rather rude and flippant remark to one of our daughters in front of other customers. She was left speechless and made to feel extremely unimportant. The second event occurred shortly thereafter when the same employee made an error in quoting a foreign exchange rate on a rather large transaction, an error that would have cost more than $3,000. When I brought the error to his attention, the employee argued with me, blaming the bank's computer system. In a classic customer response, I think what angered me the most was that the employee did not even offer an apology for the mistake.

The combination of the two events created such upset that, within a couple of months, my wife and I and all three of our daughters closed our accounts with the bank and proceeded to place all of our business with another major bank, where we were treated very well.

The original bank lost much more than the stream of earnings associated with my wife's account and mine. It lost the right to participate in any future growth, and, perhaps even more important, the bank lost the ability to grow and sustain the business of our three adult children and *their* spouses, none of whom now deals with that bank, and all of whom are young professionals, employed in high-paying jobs with many years of considerable earning power ahead of them. It is important to consider the referral and influencing power of customers who often influence or control much more than their own business.

The important lesson is, I believe, that the reason the bank lost the business has nothing at all to do with bank products or services, nothing to do with the rates being charged or paid, nothing to do with what is generally considered bank marketing. The current and future business of four families was lost because of a thoughtless comment and a failure to apologize for an error. The sad thing is that the bank made no attempt to recover or retain the business. Even sadder is the fact that, to this day, I still receive a letter each year personally signed by a senior VP of the bank, thanking me for being such a valued customer.

AN ASIDE: WHAT ABOUT *HISTORIC* CUSTOMER VALUE?

Another gap in the thinking of many firms when it comes to calculating the value of its customers is how to handle customers who have been valuable over a long time but whose value, as defined by the customer database or information system, is slipping. Let me illustrate with an example that I encountered recently of a retired senior multinational corporate executive who, after driving literally millions of dollars of personal, corporate, and group business to an international airline over 30 years, now is not even permitted entry to their business class lounge because he is deemed to be of no *value,* as defined by their frequent-flyer program. Over the course of a week, I heard him tell at least six different individuals and groups the story of why he will never fly that airline again.

This example reflects a number of critical points that relate to the knowledge we have about customers and how we use that knowledge. This customer had been very loyal and very valuable for many years, bringing the company millions in revenue. Because the information system or frequent-flyer program indicates that he is not flying as often and is no longer valuable, he is treated differently, creating all manner of negative effects. The airline has, in fact, created a terrorist. Not only will he never fly with the airline again, but he will tell everyone who cares to listen what a bunch of ingrates they are. The airline has lost an opportunity to create an ambassador, simply because of how it manages data and uses it to make customer decisions. It's a clear case of what a colleague of mine cogently referred to as data over-ruling marketing logic. Maybe we should be giving some greater consideration to a concept that we might label *historic customer value,* recognizing the volume of business that customers have brought us over the years and rewarding them for their loyalty. Don't we owe loyal customers something, even after they no longer show up on our data-driven most valuable customer list?

This is also a great example of a situation that companies often get into when they run frequent-shopper programs: What to do with customers who slip to a lower spend level and, as a result, are deemed to be less "valuable"? Do we reduce the benefits to which they are entitled, thereby running the risk of offending them and putting future business at risk? Or do we "grand-father" them and demonstrate how much we have appreciated their business over the years? I'd opt for the latter.

DANGER OF THE DATABASE VIEW

The database view of CLV causes firms to have a very narrow perspective on the value of customers. As with many such metrics, it's internal, historic, monetary, revenue based, and direct, and involves only what we are able to measure (see Exhibit 7.2). It is not useful where we don't have customer data.

But let's also ask why we are setting out to calculate CLV in the first place. In many firms, it is because we plan to *tailor* our marketing effort to the various value segments. In short, we will lavish attention on the profitable customers, making personal calls on them and inviting them to all manner of sporting events. We will call much less frequently on, and may even consider firing, those customers who are not pulling their weight.

There is an important paradox at work here. If we base our investment in future marketing efforts on historic sales or profitability, we will never grow the business of the less-valuable customers. Such a view of the world often leads to a misallocation of resources. If we decide that the volume of business we are receiving from them is too small to warrant paying them much attention, why would we really expect them to buy *more* from us in the future? Dipping into the database to calculate customer value and then to allocate customers to various value segments is a dangerous game. I'd want to be pretty confident in the accuracy of my data, because the danger of mis-classifying the customer is great indeed.

Exhibit 7.2   Calculating Long-Term Customer Value

The current approach tends to be . . .

- **INTERNAL** — based on easily captured internal data
- **HISTORIC** — looks at what the customer has spent in the past
- **MONETARY** — looks at value in strictly monetary terms
- **REVENUE-BASED** — relies on easily measured sales revenues
- **DIRECT** — looks only at sales the customer brings us directly

In the future, companies should consider measures that are . . .

- **EXTERNAL** — goes beyond information that is automatically captured
- **FUTURE-LOOKING** — considers the customer's potential for growth
- **NONMONETARY** — considers other forms of payback such as referrals
- **COST-BASED** — takes into account what it costs to serve the customer
- **INDIRECT** — considers business that the customer can influence

---

I observed exactly this effect a few years ago when working on a project in the veterinary pharmaceuticals industry. The client had allocated the many veterinary clinics it served into A, B, C, and D segments, based on total revenue over the preceding three years or so. It then proceeded to tailor its customer contact strategy to the segmentation, indicating that A clinics would be called on monthly by sales reps while the D clinics would receive only e-mail contact and the occasional newsletter. The move was met with opposition, not only from some of the veterinarians involved, who resented not now receiving the personal attention they had received in the past, but also from the client's own sales force, who were able to identify immediately some clinics that had been categorized as C or D that actually influenced a great deal of business from the farmers and producers they served and were a lot more valuable than sales data indicated.

The reliance of historic customer data to calculate CLV has led Edward Malthouse and Robert Blattberg to observe: "Historic value is not a very good predictor of future value. In situations where the future cannot be predicted accurately, an organization that invests a disproportionate amount of marketing resources in historically valuable customers may be investing in the wrong customers."[4]

YOU DON'T WANT THEM ALL, BUT TREAD CAREFULLY

What should be obvious by now is the fact that, if we look only at estimates of the financial value of a customer to the firm, we are potentially missing a complete picture of true customer value. But don't get the impression that all customers are valuable. Not all customers represent the same value to your firm. There are some you don't want to deal with for a variety of reasons. Some are literally more trouble than they are worth. Others don't look especially good in the portfolio. But deciding which ones to drop is not easy. You have to make the decision for the right reason.

If we are going to protect customer relationships, then we should start with protecting those that have the greatest potential future value. But many firms do not know where to begin in assessing customer value. Or they do it too narrowly. The principle is solid, but we may not know who is really valuable.

Attempting to deliver a level of customer service appropriate to a customer's estimated value is a risky strategy. In the first place, unless the company has very good information on the true value of the customer, there is a very real risk that it could be wrong in labeling a customer low value. In such a situation, the strategy adopted to "serve" the low-value customer may involve reducing service levels to the point where the customer may decide to take her business elsewhere, or charging fees or higher prices to such customers so that they become profitable or are encouraged to leave. The danger, of course, is that the firm may offend customers who are in fact more valuable than available data may indicate, or create a public relations problem because customers voice publicly their views on how they are being treated. This short-term view of the value of customers is potentially damaging to a firm's future revenue streams.

At first glance, the idea of helping or encouraging customers to take their business elsewhere seems a rather harsh step to take and one that may backfire on a company; however, it can be a means to improved profitability for the company and higher-quality service for the best customers. Shedding those customers who are genuinely not paying their way makes considerable business sense, provided you are confident that you are identifying them correctly. One critical problem, however, is that most businesses are ill-equipped to identify such customers accurately.

WHAT'S IMPORTANT?

A number of lessons learned from this chapter merit emphasis at this point. Calculating or in some way getting a handle on the long-term value of a customer is important for a firm. First, it demonstrates to employees that the firm is focused on cultivating customer relationships so as to maximize the long-term payback that flows from them. It sends a very important message that, by engaging in behavior that in any way puts customer relationships at risk, the employee is jeopardizing a very important flow of revenue, not only from the customer directly but from any business that he or she might influence.

Second, determining the long-term value of a customer may influence decisions concerning those customers with whom the company wishes to establish and maintain relationships. Once a concerted effort is made to place a value on a customer relationship, a firm may be able to identify those customers whose long-term potential is very good and those with whom profitable relationships are not likely to be formed. The firm can better target its resources toward establishing and maintaining those customer relationships that have the greatest potential for payback.

Calculating the value of a customer relationship or the payback to be obtained from that relationship is not easy. Many companies simply do not have the information available to do it properly, and some seem disinclined to embark on the process, possibly because they do not appreciate the value of the results. Most companies, however, can develop an approach that would represent a good approximation, provided that it includes an attempt to calculate less obvious aspects of relationship value, including the future potential of customers, the nonmonetary benefits to be gained through association with them, and their potential to influence the business of others.

Chances are you are still thinking "How can I measure some of the things discussed in this chapter?" You still need to know if your customer relationship strategy is working, and it would be great to be able to get a better handle on the long-term value of your customers. We'll turn our attention to measurement in Chapter 8, addressing the important customer-focused metrics you need and how you actually can collect them.

Endnotes

1. Frederick F. Reichheld and W. Earl Sasser Jr., "Zero Defections: Quality Comes to Services," *Harvard Business Review* (September–October 1990): 105–111.

2. Ibid.

3. Frederick F. Reichheld, "The One Number You Need to Grow," *Harvard Business Review* 81, no. 12 (December 2003): 46–54.

4. Edward C. Malthouse and Robert C. Blattberg, "Can We Predict Customer Lifetime Value?" *Journal of Interactive Marketing* 19, no. 1 (Winter 2005): 14.

8

HOW ARE YOU DOING?

We now turn our attention to the challenging issue of knowing how well you are doing in your quest to establish more meaningful relationships with your customers. But first we need to revisit the concept of customer insight that we raised briefly in Chapter 1. It must be obvious, if a firm is to develop an effective customer strategy, that the strategy must be grounded in much more insightful information than is typically available. We discuss in some detail how that insight into the customer might be obtained. Then we address the burning question of whether customers are noticing your efforts to establish an emotional connection. Is the strategy working? Are you having the desired effect of building a closer attachment between your brand and your customers? We have to know this if we are going to be able to evaluate the strategy and refine it as we move forward.

CHARACTERISTICS OF RELATIONSHIP-FOCUSED FIRMS

I have concluded that, in order for a firm to be truly relationship focused, it must exhibit four characteristics.

1. **It must take a long-term view of customer relationships.** It must subscribe to the perspective that relationships cannot be built overnight and that the achievement of relationship status with customers involves more than meeting short-term sales and profit targets.

2. **The firm must accept the fact that the customer defines the relationship.** It is the customer, not the firm, who decides when a relationship is in place. This is a revelation to many firms, which persist in the view that they can decide with whom to have a relationship

and on what terms. Many believe they have relationships with customers while customers laugh at the idea.

3. **It will readily agree that a relationship is an emotional concept and that customer relationships involve an emotional connection with the firm.** Once they accept this view, companies immediately realize that they cannot build relationships simply on the strength of product quality and functional performance, which are, as researchers observe, necessary but not sufficient.

4. **It must accept that it must change its approach to measuring organizational success.** Most companies have evolved, relying on conventional accounting-based measures of corporate performance. These "hard" measures must be supplemented by a series of "soft" measures that reflect the firm's ability to establish and maintain customer relationships.

Firms that embrace the objective of establishing a connection with their customers must also move beyond conventional marketing metrics to assess how well they are doing in meeting customer needs and in creating that connection. Many firms are using data and customer information that are inadequate to the task of guiding the development of a customer strategy.

What we have been addressing in this book isn't conventional marketing; it's more powerful than that, more holistic, more all-encompassing. Simply put, we *must* get the marketing right. But, marketing covers only a part of what contributes to a customer's decision to buy or not to buy, to stay or not to stay. The customer purchase and patronage decision is a multilayered, multistage, multifaceted one. Insightful research and casual conversations with customers will reveal that much of what causes them to buy or not has nothing to do with the conventional marketing mix. The product is increasingly of high quality, the price is attractive, it's made available in a convenient and timely way, and the necessary information has been communicated. Marketing has done its job, but the deal falls through and the customer leaves. Why?

Businesses must move beyond the view that the marketing department is solely responsible for the firm's success with customers. The conventional marketing mix represents the things that you have to get done and get done well. But it's not enough. As we have been discussing throughout this book, the factors that will likely cement a long-lasting customer relationship are those that drive the emotional attachment to the company. These are generally much softer.

In this chapter we address the fact that your firm needs insight into the lives of your customers in order to prepare an effective customer strategy. We also explore new kinds of measures that you will need to use if you are to determine the effectiveness of that strategy. Insight is needed to drive strategy; new and different metrics are needed to evaluate performance and to refine the strategy.

20/20 INSIGHT

Why do we need customer insight, and how do we know when we have found it? Essentially, we need to delve more deeply inside the minds and lives of customers to reveal ideas that can turn into opportunities to impress them and to set ourselves apart from competitors by behaving differently. When I set out to reveal customer insight for clients, I am not specifically looking for new product ideas or for ways that the firm can push more products. I am looking for ideas that will allow the firm to change the way it interacts with customers and how it behaves toward them, thereby building that elusive emotional connection. This is much more of what is now being viewed as a "pull" approach to the customer.

To be truly insightful, information that is obtained from customers must meet two criteria:

1. **It has to tell us something that we didn't already know.** My reaction, when I hear a customer say something that I haven't heard before, is often "Wow! Where is that coming from?" In other words, it has to be new information that surprises us because it causes us to think in a different direction. It's disruptive in that it shakes us from our conventional view of the customer and gives us reason to explore new directions. It starts us thinking about how we can use that insight to create an improved customer experience or do something unexpected that will truly impress.

2. **It has to be actionable.** It must point us in a direction that will allow the firm to add a new kind of value for customers. It has to be relevant to the environment in which the customer and the company meet. It must provide the firm with ideas that will allow for the meaningful addition of value. It's not insightful information if it does not pertain to an aspect of the customer's life in which the company may become legitimately involved.

Don't make the mistake of believing that insight is difficult to find. It often isn't. I rarely participate in a focus group or one-on-one interview that doesn't reveal at least one or two nuggets of information that point the client in a new direction or reveal an opportunity that is worth pursuing. That is not to say that anyone can obtain such insight. It is not as simple as sitting down and having a conversation with customers, although such situations may indeed reveal gems of wisdom. Gaining insight generally is not that easy, and usually an experienced professional must be involved to get the greatest value out of the exercise.

NOT ABOUT MINING AND SURVEYING

There are many ways to obtain the kind of unstructured information that can prove truly insightful. Much has been written about the ability to obtain insight from customer data. No doubt that is where many companies find the insight they are looking for, but it isn't necessarily the kind of customer insight I am talking about.

The overabundance of data that is captured automatically by many businesses represents an embarrassment of riches. Although it is something of a paradox to suggest that the more data we have on customers, the less we really know them, that seems to be the case, as some firms have deliberately reduced the amount of customer research they are doing in favor of mining their customer databases. No amount of mining activity, involving as it does the application of predictive modeling and other tools, will ever tell us *why*. Databases contain extremely detailed data on customer purchases: what they buy and when, returns, prices paid, time of day, and other information. Some also contain reasonably up-to-date demographic information about the customer and the household; those that have been able to link or integrate databases have added online behavior, incorporating information on Web pages visited, click-through behavior, transactions completed, and sites abandoned.

I'm not suggesting that such information is not valuable; it is, primarily for tactical decision making. It isn't particularly helpful in driving a customer strategy simply because it limits our understanding of the customer to behavioral information and possibly some demographics. It tells us what the customer has done and allows us to predict with some high degree of statistical accuracy what she is likely to buy next or more of. It can, therefore, direct better-targeted marketing campaigns and more efficient allocation of resources. But it simply doesn't tell us why the customer is acting as she is or how she feels about her dealings with the firm.

To obtain the kind of valuable, strategy-driving insight we need, we can't avoid talking with people. We need to probe deeply into customers' thought processes, their lives, and what I keep referring to as the context in which they are operating. This can be done only through relatively unstructured conversation. Customer surveys can produce a certain amount of valuable information on specific topics but rarely reveal insight, simply because the customer is restricted to responding to researcher-designed questions rather than being able to inject his own thoughts. Even when so-called verbatim comments are recorded during customer surveys, they are typically "collapsed" into convenient coding categories for reporting purposes.

GO DEEP!

You need to know more about your customers. Depending on the project, I would want to know how they spend their weekends, what constitutes an ideal vacation or shopping trip, what they do to relax, what books they are reading, what challenges they are facing, what they are looking forward to in the next few years, what they dread happening, what literally keeps them awake at night, and what they are passionate about. I would also want to know how they feel about dealing with your firm and with your competitors, what they like about you and what they really dislike, what usually goes right and what occasionally goes wrong, and whether they like dealing with some employees and not others.

In a business-to-business (B2B) setting, the questions would be different, but still oriented toward revealing information that may be only peripherally related to the client's business. We need to know what customers expect to happen in their industry or market in the next two or three years, what are the most difficult challenges they face today, who they like to see call on them, what they dread, what they hate to see on their desks when they arrive at work on Monday morning, and the inevitable, what keeps them awake at night.

Of course, this is not an exhaustive list of the questions I would suggest you ask your customers. But it reflects the kind of conversation that will produce the insight needed to reveal ideas that are worth pursuing. For example, in retailing research, customers often say that they feel "uncomfortable" shopping at certain retail stores. But how often do we dig deeply into exactly what customers mean when they make such a comment? When we do probe, we find that comfort in this context has little if anything to do with physical comfort but a great deal more to do with whether they feel that they fit with the clientele that typically frequents that store and with how they are viewed and made to feel by staff and other shoppers. It's a very emotional concept and one that retailers must understand if they are to create the right atmosphere or ambiance to make customers feel comfortable shopping in their stores.

WHERE TO GO FOR INSIGHT

There are many ways to obtain this kind of information, starting with two approaches that have been used by conventional researches for many years. Focus groups and one-on-one interviews can be extremely productive in revealing the kind of customer information you need, provided they are conducted properly. There is much debate in corporate and research circles on the value of focus groups. In these days of Internet surveys, relational databases, and predictive modeling, some see focus groups as a relic of the past. But as Barry Watson of Environics Research observed recently,

> *"Because that [Internet and database analysis] is so detached from the individuals, it's going to put more onus on having mechanisms to really just put a face on the consumers that we're trying to understand. . . . [Q]ualitative research is going to become more important as we depend more on these other sources."*[1]

One of the principal reasons that this debate is being waged is that many focus groups are done badly. The technique has become so commonplace in recent years that everyone thinks that he or she can do a focus group. Many companies have taken to doing their own, bringing in 8 or 10 customers for lunch, chatting with them for an hour or so, and calling it a focus group. It isn't. Focus groups are not things that we casually pull together to see what we might find out. They are an extremely valuable form of research—if done well. To be done well, they must be planned carefully and, above all, led by a moderator who has a lot of experience and understands how to get the most out of the technique.

In certain situations, meeting customers in one-on-one interviews is more practical and productive than trying to get eight together for a focus group. This is likely to be the case with B2B customers, where it may be difficult to convene a group and where some participants may not want to share their information in front of others. The one-on-one in-depth interview also works very well when customers are being asked to discuss personal subjects and where the content of the interview is likely to be very complex.

Regardless of whether customers are being interviewed in a group or individually, obtaining the kind of insight we have been discussing requires that the interview be planned so as to ensure that all pertinent topics are covered. I typically prepare, in close consultation with the client, an interview guide that maps out where the interview must go, leaving room for flexibility to explore interesting side roads as they reveal themselves. I generally start with a discussion relating to some of the very broad subjects mentioned earlier, the "What's going on in your industry these days?" kind of questions. Gradually, over the course of two hours or more, we move through increasingly more targeted discussion, ending with specific questions relating to the client's business and what customers like and dislike about it.

In recent years, some companies have turned to researchers to conduct different forms of qualitative research, involving techniques that have their roots in sociology and ethnography. We are seeing greater use of so-called day-in-the-life research, where one or more researchers, often accompanied by a video crew, literally spend a full day or more in the homes or offices of customers, observing and asking probing questions.

MORE STRUCTURED SOURCES

Some companies have formalized the gathering of customer insight by organizing customer panels, customer councils, or customer advisory boards. Some companies will have more than one, with each representing a different segment of customers or a different division of the business. The purpose of such panels is simply to provide feedback to the firm. While many are oriented toward the testing of new product ideas, many are being used more creatively to provide companies with a view inside the customer's mind that they simply can't get through survey research. Most customer councils have been face-to-face affairs, but some companies are now organizing online customer communities and blogs to obtain the unfettered information they crave.

The difference between qualitative research and customer panels or councils is that the former is typically done by an experienced professional while the latter is usually organized and managed by the firm itself. Focus groups and one-on-one interviews are more likely to reveal less biased information, but customer panels have their own unique value to the firm, not least of which is the sense of involvement that they convey to customers, reinforcing the feeling of ownership that is so important in relationship building. Customers who are involved in such projects often say how much they appreciate that the company is asking them for their opinion.

Many larger companies, such as Southwest Airlines, John Deere, and Harley-Davidson, have operated customer panels and dealer advisory councils for many years with great results. LEGO, the toy maker, launched its Ambassadors Program to obtain insightful information from adult enthusiasts for the unique LEGO product line. The 15 to 20 "ambassadors" provide feedback on new product ideas as they are being developed and represent a valuable connection between the company and its most supportive and influential customers. As Jake McKee, LEGO's global community relations specialist, observed, "Our company has recognized the benefit of direct customer dialogue. We're not selling products in the Ambassadors Program or looking to participants to push products for us. In their involvement with the company, we can demonstrate respect for our customers; and both sides get something out of the relationship. They're real people, and we want them to be happy with LEGO Group and our products."[2]

PLAN TO MEASURE RESULTS

Even before you have your customer strategy developed and implemented, you must turn your attention to how you plan to measure performance against the strategy. How will you assess whether your customer strategy is working? How will you know if you are strengthening the emotional connection, the relationships with your customers? Obtaining the information you need to assess the state of the relationship is not a simple task. Getting agreement on what you need to measure is itself a formidable challenge.

Two very interesting and potentially conflicting things have been happening in management in recent years that have implications for how we determine the success of our customer strategy. First, managers at all levels in organizations are being pressured to demonstrate the (usually financial) success of their initiatives, even to the point, as mentioned in Chapter 7, of producing accurate calculations of return on investment (ROI). Second, progressive companies have for the most part accepted the logic of increasing levels of customer service and retention, and speak with some sense of pride of their efforts to build customer relationships. Many companies wrestle with the issue of trying to put numbers on the quality or strength of their relationships with customers.

CHALLENGES OF BEING ACCOUNTABLE

There exists tremendous pressure to justify expenditures, even on "soft" initiatives such as employee training and customer relationship building.

This pressure to measure comes not only from the need to keep costs down so as to achieve short-term financial performance targets, but also because it is believed we can measure just about anything these days. Companies suffer from the technologicalization of customer knowledge. We have data on everything. Surely we can use that data to calculate whether we are being successful.

In most large companies at least, corporate performance is assessed by reference to conventional, accounting-based numbers. We rely on what I have referred to as a FISH approach, in that these measures of success are almost always *f*inancial, *i*nternal, *s*hort term, and *h*istoric in nature. We look to sales, earnings per share, return on equity, and other such measures to determine whether a company has been successful and whether senior management should be rewarded for that success.

But it takes some time for the results of a customer strategy to begin to influence these numbers. A constant organizational striving for short-term financial results conspires against a long-term customer-focused strategy. Before a firm can develop that strategy and before it can begin to assess its success, there has to be acceptance within the management ranks of the company of the legitimacy of such a focus, reflected in a different approach to the measurement of corporate performance.

We see the same tendency to wish to quantify immediate results in marketing and in the management of call centers. We look for the return on individual campaigns in terms of their ability to drive short-term sales and increase market share. Contact centers are, for the most part, focused on operational efficiencies, throughput, calls per agent, speed to serve, wait time, and so forth. These are all input measures and are all about us, not the customer. We are trying to optimize return on spend. We are usually not capturing the effect of such efforts on customer relationships and on the creation of negative emotional responses.

For many firms, the kind of strategy outlined in this book will represent a departure from the regular way of doing business. This is not a conventional way of managing; we don't have an accepted set of measures. Demonstrating the connection between the kinds of initiatives that we have referred to and the ultimate effect on the financial performance of the company is a challenge, especially when senior executives, boards of directors, and financial analysts may not be prepared to wait. They want immediate results. We need to be able to show that there is a payback from delivering a helium balloon with a child's first bed and from offering to have a suitcase repaired for a regular hotel guest. We can easily measure the cost of doing such things, but measuring the effect is difficult.

ACCEPTING THE NEED TO MEASURE

Companies that intend to implement a customer strategy must accept that there is a need to know that the strategy is working and that conventional corporate and marketing measures are inadequate to the task, principally because they are short term in nature and tend to measure primarily financial and behavioral numbers. Strategy making is, by definition, a long-term prospect. It will take two or three years for your firm to realize its investment in its customer strategy. How do you keep the dollar watchers happy in the meantime? Essentially, you need to be able to demonstrate that key indicators of relationship health are moving in the right direction and to show the connection between those key measures and the FISH measures we talked about earlier. We need to prove that, by implementing the kind of strategy we have been discussing in this book, we will drive marketing-related behavioral measures like store traffic, spend, frequency of buying, and share of wallet, and we will affect positively key corporate performance measures such as sales and profitability.

Many companies today are facing a critical duality: They are being asked to be more efficient and to deliver an acceptable ROI on "soft" things yet, at the same time, customers are much more demanding of better treatment and are increasingly impressed by those companies that treat them special, and are prepared to reward them with their loyalty. We hear a great deal in most companies about the need to increase productivity and to contain costs while doing so. Yet many firms also accept that increased customization and personalization of service will ultimately drive customer loyalty. There is a growing acceptance of the validity of a long-term view of the customer and of the need to implement strategies that are intended to drive retention and even relationships.

It is critical, therefore, that both of these seemingly conflicting approaches to doing business be reflected in your measurement program. How you measure the success of your relationship building initiatives must reflect the impact they are having on building an emotional connection with customers and the effect of that enhanced connection on conventional financial and behavioural measures. You need to have two parallel and equally important streams of thought operating at all times. Proponents on each side of the debate must accept the legitimacy of the other and the fact that they have to be linked.

WE *CAN* MEASURE THIS

I am often challenged by managers who suggest that one can't measure relationships, or emotional attachment, or customer experience; these are considered soft and fuzzy concepts, and managers are accustomed to working with measures that are hard and financial. My answer, of course, is that we *can* measure such things.

Essentially, the challenge is to provide evidence that the customer strategy that we are implementing is having a positive effect on improving the experience for the customer, on creating positive emotions, on building the emotional connection, and on establishing solid relationships—*and* that all of this will, over time, drive changes in the behavioral and financial measures on which managers are so dependent.

We can get some direction concerning what we need to measure from the model discussed in this book and from the critical components of the customer strategy framework. Recall from Chapter 2 that we identified five levels of our *drivers of customer relationships* model. An integrated measurement program would ensure that we have solid, well-developed measures of how well we are doing at each of these levels. In fact, much conventional marketing research already addresses the first three levels. Most companies that are interested in assessing how well they are doing in appealing to their customers will periodically evaluate their performance on core aspects of the value proposition, the core product or service, how well it is being delivered, whether customers are satisfied with the provision of service, and whether the company's systems and processes are working well.

It is at the top two levels of our drivers model that we need to add new measures, those that typically have not been addressed. These relate to how customers feel about their interaction with the company and its people, the experience that's involved, and the ultimate emotional connection, how they feel toward the firm and their dealings with it.

We can get some additional direction regarding what should be measured to enable us to evaluate the implementation of the customer strategy by examining the essential components of our framework. Therefore, we need to better understand how successful we have been in meeting and exceeding *customer expectations,* including whether we have been able to surprise them from time to time. We need to know how well we have been creating both functional and emotional *value* for our customers. We need to determine the extent to which we have been creating both negative and positive *emotions* and the degree of intensity of each. And, finally, we need to know how successful we have been at creating positive *customer experiences,* including not only their experience in dealing with us and our people but also the extent to which we have been seen to be contributing to and enabling other experiences.

This sounds like a complex undertaking, and it is. Concepts like customer relationships and emotional connection are deep, complex emotive concepts; they can't be measured superficially or simplistically. You also can't get a true picture of how well you are doing with your customer strategy by examining existing customer data. By the same token, measuring emotional connection and customer relationships is not the same as measuring some more conventional marketing constructs, such as brand attitudes, satisfaction, or involvement.[3] I routinely hear managers suggest that they don't need to delve more deeply because they already do customer satisfaction research. As concluded in Chapter 2, satisfaction is not a relationship, and measuring satisfaction is far too simplistic an approach to evaluating something as complex as the customer strategy we have been building.

MEASURING THE EQUITY IN THE RELATIONSHIP

I have for many years been intrigued by the fact that one of a firm's most valuable assets—the accumulated relationships that the company or brand has with its loyal customers—never appears on the balance sheet, and most firms typically do not attempt to place a value on it. In most firms, it is an asset that is very much taken for granted. While it is easy for executives and investors to visualize tangible and financial assets, it is much more difficult to understand concepts as amorphous as loyalty or relationships. But they are of immense value and represent the future earnings of the firm. Any attempt to develop measures of such assets will often be met with some resistance because we are asking managers and executives to consider measures with which they are unfamiliar and likely uncomfortable.

This book is essentially about taking a different approach to corporate growth, by doing creative things to build an emotional connection with customers that will drive long-term revenue flow, through increased share of spend and positive referrals. Therefore, we need to use new and different measures if we are to be successful in evaluating how well we are doing.

Some years ago, realizing that we needed a set of "soft," nonfinancial, customer-based, long-term, forward-looking metrics to complement what most firms already have, which are typically "harder" and oriented toward the needs of finance departments and the investment community, I developed such a measure, the BREI (Barnes Relationship Equity Index). Such a measure would have to be a very good predictor of customer behavior (which is the principal interest of marketing folks) and of higher-level corporate performance indicators (the financial, internal, short-term historic measures referred to earlier). I created the BREI by analyzing in great detail what customers across many industries had been telling my research colleagues and I for many years, and by examining how social psychologists and other social scientists have been measuring soft, emotive concepts for many years. It is a soft-centered, multidimensional measure that allows a firm to take the pulse of its customer relationships and to determine the extent to which it has been successful in establishing an emotional connection with various segments of its customer base.

The BREI is typically administered to a sample of customers through a telephone survey but is increasingly being conducted over the Internet, involving a questionnaire that consists of several components. In addition to predictable questions relating to satisfaction and self-report behavior toward the company and its brands, this survey addresses specific areas that allow us to measure how well we are doing in the areas that characterize the customer strategy.

One of the most obvious conclusions to be drawn from social psychology is that a relationship is a multidimensional construct. If it is to be measured, it has to be approached as a series of relevant dimensions. It is necessary to deconstruct a customer's relationship with a company or brand into a series of components that one would associate with any kind of relationship, whether interpersonal or otherwise. To measure customer relationships, we must measure the dimensions of those relationships.

The BREI survey involves capturing customers' ratings of the firm on important dimensions of the relationship, including trust, communications, sense of community, respect, understanding, commitment, and attachment. A typical customer survey involves calculation of scores on as many as 12 relationship dimensions.

We also need to know how well the firm is doing in terms of creating various forms of value, both functional and emotional, for customers. Through research across industries, we have identified several forms of value that are instrumental as drivers of long-term relationships. Through the survey, we measure the extent to which the firm is creating each.

The survey also explores the critical area of customer experiences, assessing how well the firm is delivering on the four forms of experience identified in Chapter 5. Finally, we calculate a component that is labeled "emotional tone," as it captures the extent to which the firm is creating a series of negative and positive emotions in its dealings with its customers.

The application of the BREI methodology gives us insight into the factors that contribute to the creation of genuine customer relationships, how a company is performing in terms of creating such relationships with its customers, where those relationships are weak and where they are strong, and what actions are likely to prove most effective in improving relationships in the future. By using a consistent approach to calculating the BREI, we create a weighted composite index of the overall strength of the customer relationship. This index, which is typically reported on a 100-point scale, is comparable across customer segments and allows the firm to track performance over time in improving its customer relationships.

Thus, a BREI score for a company or brand embodies the health of the relationship that the company currently enjoys with its customer base and with various segments within it. A company that scores above 80 across its customer base, for example, is doing very well in establishing an emotional connection and has a very solid relationship. A company whose BREI score is 62, however, has a lot of work to do.

CONNECTING TO HARDER NUMBERS

Companies today, with the help of technology, do a good job of capturing the hard numbers, so the big challenge is to link the softer BREI to the harder marketing and financial measures. Most larger companies have volumes of customer data available, and this represents an advantage when we set out to prove the financial payback to the firm of establishing solid customer relationships.

Where we have access to customer data and are able to track behavioral measures such as total spend, share of spend, frequency of patronage, purchases at full price, and customer profitability, we can demonstrate through the BREI the effectiveness of building a positive relationship and a strong emotional connection. By merging BREI survey results with customer database data, we are able to show the state of the relationship by customer segment and can prove that those with the highest levels of relationship scores will clearly deliver impressive numbers for the firm.

Reanalysis of data from projects over the past 10 years shows that those customers whose BREI score is above 80, compared with those whose score is between 60 and 80, will deliver to the firm approximately 10 percent higher share of wallet, will be 30 percent more likely to remain as customers and not to defect to the competition, and will be more than 50 percent more likely to recommend the company or brand to their friends and associates.

Over time, companies with very high BREI scores will reduce customer churn, will sell more at full price, thus realizing higher margins, will drive profitability, and ultimately will increase share price.

RELATIONSHIP SEGMENTATION

With BREI, we are now able to add a relationship quality variable to a company's segmentation exercise and develop a relationship segmentation strategy. In other words, we enhance greatly the insight that a company can bring to segmentation, thereby allowing it to move beyond conventional demographic and product usage approaches.

We can show the value to the firm of various customer segments in terms of the strength of their relationship. A segment with an average BREI score of 87 would likely warrant a strategy that is characterized as maintenance or protection, with the company making sure that it looks after this segment very well and does nothing to jeopardize the relationship. However, a segment that produces a BREI of 42 may warrant little attention as the likelihood of moving that score into the 60-plus range may be limited. For all segments that are identified, detailed diagnostics are produced that identify where the relationship is weak and where it is strong and which particular components of the BREI are driving the overall score. Analysis provides the direction for corrective action to be taken. We can determine which segments are priorities for the firm, what each segment is currently worth to the company, and how solid the business is.

We can also place a value on the relationship with each segment so that the firm can determine the value of taking corrective action. Being able to assess the size and value of each segment allows the firm to set more than behavioral and financial goals. For example, the BREI analysis may reveal a segment with considerable growth potential, where the company's goal may be to drive the BREI from 72 to 75 within the next two years. We can calculate the payback from succeeding because we can place a financial value on each point on the BREI scale.

RELATIONSHIPS AT RISK

An extremely valuable by-product of the measurement of customer relationship quality is the ability to diagnose relationship weaknesses. Relationships are constantly ebbing and flowing; they are a work in progress, and we need to know where we stand. We should be able to tell where and with whom relationships are weak and where they are strong. We should then be pointed in the right direction to shore up the weaknesses. Ongoing monitoring of relationship quality will reveal early warning signs of relationship deterioration, allowing you to spot when things are in danger of going off the rails and with whom. It also allows you to monitor how well you are doing in managing distant and technology-based relationships where the opportunity to meet the customer is very infrequent.

Relationships are potentially very vulnerable in a number of situations in the course of a firm's dealings with its customers. These occasions usually involve a break point or a hiatus in a relationship; something happens that has the potential to disrupt the relationship and may provide an opportunity for the customer to try someone else. Such occasions occur when customers move from one town or neighborhood to another; when the employee who has been looking after their business retires, is transferred, or goes on maternity leave; when branch offices are closed; and when brands are discontinued or undergo changes in formulation. In situations like this, a company needs a relationship transition strategy and needs to monitor how successful it has been in migrating the relationship from one employee to another and through the transition period.

Auto dealerships provide an interesting example of a situation where a relationship goes through a transition. A very large percentage of vehicles are now leased though dealerships, and by definition the dealer and leasing company know exactly when a lease is to expire. Yet, I am told, well under 50 percent of auto leases are rolled over in most dealerships. That is, far less than 50 percent of drivers lease another car from the same dealer. The lease expiry represents a break point in the relationship, one that must be managed well if the customer is to lease again.

An examination of the process by which lease transition is managed may provide a clue as to why more drivers do not continue to lease with the same dealer. Communication with the customer is typically initiated by the leasing company (not the dealer!) several months before the lease is to expire. That communication is usually in the form of a very procedural letter that outlines the steps the customer must follow either to return the vehicle or to arrange to buy out the lease. Examples that I have seen go into great detail to explain how the customer must ensure that the vehicle is returned in good condition, how the customer must pay to repair dents larger that a certain size—even conveniently providing a template so the customer can measure the size of any "dings" in the doors. One customer told me that the whole process made him feel like a criminal rather than a valued customer.

BENEATH THE RADAR:
THE PROBLEM OF THE "ALMOST CUSTOMER"

There is one aspect of customer strategy that I have often thought especially difficult to deal with. That is the phenomenon of the "almost customer."[4]

I meet these almost customers regularly and they are legion. In fact, I am tempted to suggest that the almost-customer problem may be as important as customer churn for some companies. The problem is that we are unable to measure just how important it is.

I am sure you have been an almost customer on many occasions. You see a very nice coat in a shop window, but when you go in to buy it, you can't find anyone to serve you, or the salesperson is decidedly unhelpful, or he doesn't offer to see if their downtown store has your size. You leave, totally frustrated. You call the sales department of a local company to place an order, only to be put on hold. Twenty minutes later, you hang up in disgust. You try to buy an attractive garden bench online only to be thwarted by a very user-unfriendly and frustrating Web site.

What's happening here? You really did want to buy, you had your credit card out, you had made up your mind. Marketing had done its work. But something happened to turn you off or to make it impossible for you to consummate the deal. You are totally frustrated, angry, and disappointed because you really did want to buy that coat.

Businesses routinely drive customers away before they have even become customers. They are nipping a potential relationship in the bud before it has a chance to get started. It makes little sense to talk of cementing meaningful or genuine customer relationships if we are unable to get the customer on the books or into the database for the first time.

This subject of the almost customer is relevant to all businesses in the context of developing the customer strategy. I am firmly convinced that it results in millions of dollars of lost business each year; business that the company does not even know it has lost. Almost customers are, by definition, virtually impossible to track. They leave no trail.

The almost-customer concept is also closely related to all of the key principles that have been discussed so far. Customer expectations are typically high in that often the customer has done her preliminary reconnaissance and has decided to buy. The work is done; it's ours to lose; expectations are dashed. Feelings play a key role in that extremely intense negative emotions often are invoked, principally because expectations were high and the experience was so unexpected. Finally, the customer literally or virtually walks out mainly because of some very negative element of the experience of dealing with the firm, not because any aspect of the conventional marketing mix failed. My research indicates that the decision to abandon the purchase is almost always a result of a problem with people, with complex processes or procedures, with unfriendly technology interface, or with what customers call stupid rules.

Customers (or, more correctly, prospective customers) are today faced with an unprecedented range of choices—not only choices of what to buy but where to buy it. The phenomenon of the almost customer is, therefore, likely to increase as customers refuse to accept shoddy treatment and simply walk out, often vowing never to return. They are clearly less willing to persevere, to tolerate, and to put up with unacceptable treatment. They will find what they are looking for elsewhere.

The underlying damage is not only that the company has lost the sale, but very likely the almost customers have also launched a torrent of negative word of mouth. Certainly these noncustomers are loath to go back, but they are not at all reluctant to tell their friends. "You'll never believe what happened to me today. They didn't have the common courtesy to . . . etc. etc."

A MEASUREMENT PLAN

The ability to measure the quality of the relationship that a firm has with its various customer groups provides not only feedback on how well the implementation of the customer strategy is going but extremely valuable information that will guide other aspects of the company's operation. For example, the calculation of the BREI index of relationship quality, combined with a similar calculation of its target customers' relationships with other firms and properties, would allow a firm to assess the potential value of planned partnerships, sponsorships, or spokesperson decisions *before* they are made. There is little point in jeopardizing your customer relationships by partnering with or sponsoring a company or event with which your customers do not have a very positive relationship.

Before you begin to formulate your customer strategy, you must address the question of measurement. You will need a measurement plan. You will also need to take the first set of measures *before* you begin to implement the customer strategy so that you have a basis of comparison as you move through implementation.

Endnotes

1. Quoted in Rebecca Harris, "Do Focus Groups Have a Future?" *Marketing Magazine Online,* June 6, 2005.
2. Michael Lowenstein, "LEGO Products Aren't Just Toys, They're an Example of How to Really Put Customers at the Heart of the Business," www.crmguru.com, November 29, 2005.

3. Matthew Thomson, Deborah J. MacInnis, and C. Whan Park, "The Ties That Bind: Measuring the Strength of Consumers' Emotional Attachment to Brands," *Journal of Consumer Psychology* 15, no. 1 (2005): 77–91.

4. James G. Barnes, Brian R. King, and Gordon A. Breen, "The Almost Customer: A Missed Opportunity to Enhance Corporate Success," *Managing Service Quality* 14, no. 2/3 (2004): 134–146.

9

WHAT MANAGEMENT NEEDS TO KNOW

It is easy to suggest that some companies just "don't get it." But *why* don't they get it? Why is it that some companies seem inherently to understand their customers and genuinely care about them, while others just don't seem to give a damn? What is it that distinguishes one group from the other? I firmly believe that the answer is very much wrapped up in how the company is led and in the culture that prevails. We may well find that the company that treats its customers best also treats its employees very well.

The kind of attitude toward the customer that is implicit in the customer strategy that we have been building cannot be imposed. It must be an organic process that is led by senior managers and eventually takes over as the prevailing ethos throughout the company. Some companies come by it naturally. We all know small neighborhood businesses that are a delight to deal with and that have succeeded in building a solid base of extremely loyal and enthusiastic advocates as customers, yet whose owners and managers may never have taken a course in marketing or read a management book on how they could become more customer focused. It's simply the kind of people they are.

IT'S A DIFFERENT VIEW OF THINGS

There are many reasons why a small grocer or dry cleaner may be able to get closer to his or her customers than a large corporation can. Yet there do exist large companies that have become role models for others and that have succeeded in establishing a meaningful connection with their customers. We will talk further about some of these later in this chapter. These successful companies have, for the most part, created a climate or a culture that supports and encourages a customer-focused view. It's a different philosophy, and it requires commitment from the top of the company. It's all about change management.

In many companies, it will be necessary to make changes in how the firm thinks about its customers and behaves toward them. This kind of change cannot be driven from the middle ranks of the company; it requires a total commitment from the top. I have met many midlevel managers who are totally committed to a greater emphasis on building stronger emotional connections and closer relationships with customers, only to have their best efforts thwarted by a lack of support from the senior ranks. To develop and implement an effective customer strategy, chief executive officers (CEOs) and other senior executives must appreciate the wisdom of the approach and understand the payback to be realized.

The change that is required in many companies represents a response to how customers themselves are changing. There is considerable anecdotal and research evidence that customers are rebelling against the hard sell and against aggressive marketing practices. They have far greater choices than ever before and are armed with better information. They know what they want and are not prepared to tolerate companies that don't treat them the way they want to be treated. The 2005 Yankelovich Marketing Receptivity Survey confirmed that more than half of all consumers would be willing to pay a little extra to get only the kinds of marketing they prefer. Nearly 70 percent indicated an interest in technology that would allow them to block out advertising, and 56 percent said they avoid buying products that overwhelm them with marketing and advertising.[1]

The world has changed out there, and the simple message is that many firms are going to have to change how they deal with customers or risk losing them. Many firms have recognized the value of customer retention—they come back, they spend more, and they are more valuable to us—but this retention-based view is overly simplistic. How do we get retention? The first reaction in many firms is to offer customers incentives, to bribe them. They launch yet another "customer loyalty" card, or offer price bundles, or in some other way try to influence customer buying behavior without influencing the customer's feelings toward the company or brand. The result is that they do drive retention, but only as long as their offer is better than the competition's. As soon as someone else provides a more attractive option or a card that offers more "points," retention evaporates.

The acceptance of this kind of thinking is critical if a customer strategy is to be developed and implemented successfully. Weaning a company off a singular emphasis on short-term tactics requires change in the organization, a new culture, driven from the top. It also requires a parallel stream of thinking, one based not only on short-term, financially driven goals—the FISH (financial, internal, short term, and historic) view of the world—but one that is characterized by longer-term thinking. If your company's thinking toward customers is centered around conventional push marketing, the launching of a loyalty program, or the installation of customer relationship management (CRM) systems, you need to start to change the culture before you can be successful in building an effective customer strategy. Senior managers in the firm must lead this change.

WHAT'S HOLDING US BACK?

Several characteristics of organizations and of management style conspire against allowing a firm to develop and implement a customer strategy:

- Failure to remember that customer hat.
- Succumbing to dominant logic.
- Leaning toward the hard side.
- Considering everything to be a project.
- Requiring that initiatives "show me the money."
- Letting marketing take care of that.

Remember That Customer Hat

One of the most important impediments to developing a customer strategy is a failure on the part of management to truly identify with their customers and with what they are experiencing and trying to accomplish. They simply are unable to wear their customer hats to the office. One simple exercise that may prove useful is simply to talk with your spouse and children, and ask them where they get treated really well, what their favorite stores are, what experiences they tell their friends about. Learn from them. They are customers too and they know, as all customers do, what they like and dislike. There is also nothing quite as educational and humbling for a senior executive than to pose as a customer and experience the service delivered by his or her own company.

Avoid Dominant Logic

Managers often think and behave like companies rather than like people. They are wedded to the status quo—that's the way we do things around here—

and are very slow to change. They are guilty of company think rather than customer think. Gerald Zaltman of the Harvard Business School goes so far as to suggest that "managers operate in a paradigm that prevents them from understanding and serving customers effectively."[2] They focus much more on reason than on emotions, exploring the latter only superficially. The result is that many managers tend to see customers only as a target to which they direct initiatives that will, if they are successful, result in customers buying more.

Donald Sull of the London Business School has observed that, when faced with a changing environment, including the tremendous change currently occurring in the customer marketplace, the tendency is for firms to dig in their heels and to do more of what proved successful in the past. This is what Sull has termed "active inertia."[3] The upshot of this effect is that there is a marked tendency toward the status quo, a reluctance to break out of that damned box. Companies have a sense of history and an unwillingness to abandon it.

Leaning toward the Hard Side

Most companies that I know demonstrate a natural tendency toward what I refer to as the "hard side." They are simply much more comfortable with things they can measure. As a result, they gravitate to the FISH view of the world discussed in Chapter 8 and to sales, special offers, discounts and other incentives to get customers to buy and to get them back if they have gone over to the competitor. Roger Martin, dean of the Rotman School of Management, talks about managers' natural aversion to variability.[4] This desire to have things formalized and structured means that most managers are much more comfortable with reliable, consistent, hard data than with the soft, touchy-feely task of creating emotional value.

Everything's a Project

There is also an obvious tendency in many organizations to make a project of everything. "Customer relationship management" becomes a project with a targeted date for roll-out and an implicit end date. We create teams of employees to lead such projects, leaving the impression that they have a timeline for implementation and when that's done we'll move on to other things. This is unfortunate, as it leads to an artificial structuring of customer interaction and possibly sends an unfortunate flavor-of-the-month message to employees: Once we get this CRM project done, we'll get back to normal around here. It also leads to a very functional rather than emotional view of what constitutes a relationship. In fact, CRM ought to be a commitment to a long-term change in the culture, attitude, and ethos of the company, not something we need to have done by October.

Show Me the Money

Management's focus on short-term payback often impedes a firm's ability to take a long-term view of building a customer strategy. The payback from the approach that we have been discussing will take some time to be realized, but it will come. Management's innate need to see short-term direct results from virtually everything is understandable, given the way that organizations and individuals are evaluated and rewarded. They need to be able to see the results, especially if they are being asked to provide a return on investment (ROI). But the effects of implementing a customer strategy that has as its goal the establishment of an emotional connection with customers are actually quite indirect. It's like trying to measure the effectiveness of advertising or of employee training. Because much of the payback from this strategy comes in the form of referrals and positive word of mouth, it is exceedingly difficult to obtain a direct measure of success. As a result, many companies have not been able to quantify the outcomes to the satisfaction of senior executives and boards of directors.

Let Marketing Take Care of That

Finally, it is the view in many firms that marketing owns the customer. This is a very narrow view. In fact, I could make a case that the human resources (HR) department has at least as much responsibility for customer satisfaction and for relationship building as marketing does. Much of what marketing has traditionally been all about is short term in nature, with campaigns that run for a limited time period and are designed to provide a short-term bump in sales. CRM supports this by making marketing initiatives more efficient than ever before. But a customer strategy must be much more all-encompassing and must involve every part of a company and all of its employees.

YOU NEED GREAT PEOPLE

It is impossible to implement a customer strategy without having the right people in place and without their complete support for the direction in which your firm is headed. It should be obvious that it is your people who deliver the kind of experience that will make an impression on customers. Only they are in a position to customize that experience and to seize opportunities to impress.

How do you get the team in place who can produce the results that you are looking for, who can deliver an emotional connection with customers that will represent a clear competitive advantage for your company? The first advice is to hire well. This may be your most important decision: Surround yourself with people who believe passionately in serving and impressing customers. I recall seeing a television interview a few years ago with Beverly Carmichael, vice president—people at Southwest Airlines. When she was asked to what she attributed Southwest's success, Carmichael replied, "We spend an inordinate amount of time on hiring."

McKinsey, the management consultancy, recently noted the role of employees in seizing opportunities at the "moment of truth," particularly in situations that are emotionally charged: the loss of credit cards, a canceled flight, or receipt of investment advice. The ability of employees to handle such situations and to put the customer's emotional needs ahead of the company's not only produces short-term relief or satisfaction for the customer, but actually delivers long-term financial payback to the company through increased share of wallet and customer retention. Conversely, McKinsey research shows that aggressive selling on the part of employees generates negative moments of truth and weakened corporate reputation. McKinsey's advice, first and foremost, is to hire emotionally intelligent employees, people who are born and brought up with the right emotional instincts for front-line employment.[5]

Many organizations realized some time ago that the best advice to follow is to hire on character and then teach the skills needed on the job. To deliver on the kind of customer strategy that we have been developing, it is critically important to have employees, and especially front-line employees, who can empathize with customers, who know what they are going through and trying to accomplish and who can be appropriately helpful and supportive. Employees at all levels must have a feel for the emotional content of customer interaction. They must have an innate ability to sense when negative emotions are to be avoided and to be able to seize the opportunities presented to create emotional value.

But empathy is not the only character or personality trait that I consider important. I would want colleagues and employees who are sensitive to the needs of others and who demonstrate both humility and curiosity. It takes a sense of humility to admit that the customer is often right and that the way we do things around here is not necessarily best or in the long-term best interest of the customer or, indeed, of the firm. I'd want them also to be naturally curious so that they would always be looking for unique solutions to customers' problems and unique ways to impress them. Without employees who are humble and curious, the firm is doomed to accept that what it already does is good enough.

Finally, companies that are strategically oriented toward their customers must be able to demonstrate creativity. Not everyone is naturally creative, so the firm must be prepared to put in place a climate that encourages and rewards creativity.

CREATING CREATIVITY

Chapter 6 talked about the fact that customers cannot be counted on to be particularly creative when asked how a firm might impress or surprise them. This fact creates a tremendous opportunity for companies like yours to be creative on behalf of customers. But we need people who can come up with the great ideas and a climate that encourages employees to try new and different things. Here's where we must have people who are willing to behave outside that box.

There are three components of creativity: expertise or knowledge, creative-thinking skills that have a lot to do with one's personality, and motivation.[6] It is the third component that companies can influence most easily. They can extrinsically motivate employees with material rewards, but this type of motivation can act as a constraint on creativity by causing the employee to focus on the reward rather than on the problem. It can lead employees to look for shortcuts in trying to arrive at a solution so that they will win their reward more quickly.

Creativity is often constrained because employees are always being asked to judge themselves against standards. This self-evaluation may impede creativity because people who are evaluating themselves are focused on themselves and their performance, not on new ideas. This is likely to be the case in situations where employees are constantly being observed, being made to feel self-conscious, or being evaluated. Such a workplace atmosphere may thwart creativity. An employee who must reach certain performance objectives on a regular basis is more likely to engage in an ongoing process of self-evaluation. She would constantly be focused on her performance rather than on the needs of customers and how to meet those needs creatively.

To be creative, employees must have the motivation to be creative. They must understand the role of creativity in driving some of the factors that lead to an emotional connection with customers, the most important of which is the surprise factor. Creativity is essential to surprising customers by doing things they don't experience elsewhere. Employees must understand that it is all right to be creative, that it's okay to do some different things every now and then.

Finally, in order for employees to be creative, they must have time to think. Professional firms, for example, that insist that every hour of employee time be billable to a client are unlikely to produce especially creative solutions or groundbreaking ways to impress those clients in the future.

BE CAREFUL HOW YOU PAY THEM

There exists an obvious human tendency to behave in ways that encourage rewards. Therefore, we can expect a firm's reward system to drive certain employee behavior. The simple fact is that we cannot be successful in establishing a creative, customer-focused culture in a company if we are paying people to behave otherwise. This is the case regardless of the level of the company in which an employee works. One of the reasons why senior executives are as focused as they are on short-term financial numbers is that their compensation, stock options, and bonus scheme are almost certainly tied to those numbers. This orientation is one of the most important barriers to encouraging new thinking and new behavior, particularly in large companies.

Historically, companies have paid salespeople mainly on a commission basis; if they did not sell, they did not earn. Many industries and companies, especially in the industrial sector and in certain kinds of retail, most notably auto dealers and furniture, continue to operate with this model. But in many ways driving short-term sales is inherently in conflict with the notion of building an emotional connection that will drive long-term business, especially in environments where customers are increasingly in control and in possession of all of the information they need. When customers have already decided what they want to buy and how much they are prepared to pay *before* they even go to the store or dealer, what is the role of commission-based selling?

To their credit, many companies have moved away from the straight commission basis of compensation and added a number of softer variables to the evaluation of salespeople and other employees. Some have moved toward a fairly simplistic form of measuring customer satisfaction and then linking employee pay to those results. Many customers of car dealers have experienced this uncomfortable situation, in which salespeople openly ask for a "completely satisfied" rating on the satisfaction survey.

If we want employees to contribute to the cultivation of long-term customer relationships and to create a customer environment and experience that is conducive to the establishment of that emotional connection that we have been talking about, we have to measure their performance utilizing complex measures, such as those discussed in Chapter 8, not simplistic sales and financial numbers. And we will have to reward behaviors that are going to contribute to customers being surprised and impressed and that will add emotional value. We must reward employees for what they can do for the customer, not what they can sell the customer.

GETTING THAT ELUSIVE BUY-IN

The question I get asked most often when I speak to managers and executives about building a customer strategy is: "How do I get my employees to buy in to this?" That question is often followed closely by the observation: "I wish my boss had been here to hear you." In other words, upper middle managers in particular are often frustrated that the senior executives to whom they report don't seem to "get it." At the same time, they are worried that they may not be able to get all employees in the firm thinking and acting in unison toward the common goal of enhanced customer relationships.

Let's deal first with the challenge of "selling" the notion of a customer strategy up the line to senior management. As mentioned, senior executives, particularly in larger companies, are typically focused on delivering superior financial results for their shareholders. Some will readily see the wisdom in cultivating solid customer relationships as a route to such superior corporate performance. Others will need to be convinced that spending money on the softer side of the value proposition will deliver results, especially as they are being judged on how the financials look at the end of the month or the quarter.

In my experience, to win the support of senior management for the organizational change needed, you will have to make the case for the connection between the softer side of the value proposition and the financial performance of the firm. You will need to ensure that measurement systems are in place that will allow you to demonstrate the payback to be achieved. It must be clear that there is a very definite link between the creation of emotional value for customers and the creation of financial value for the shareholders. I also find that firms' chief financial officers (CFOs) most readily accept the financial argument, as the connection between enhanced customer loyalty, reduced churn, and reduced costs are obvious.

The bigger challenge for managers and executives is likely to be getting employees at all levels of the company to appreciate the rationale for changes that are to be made and to change their behavior to be consistent with and supportive of the company's new direction. This again is where HR concepts become critically important.

The first step may be to get rid of the notion of having employees buy in. As some of my HR colleagues have suggested, the concept of buying in implies that we have to "sell" employees on doing something that they probably do not want to do or that may not even be good for them. In fact, most employees really do care about customers and find it natural to treat people well. In some companies, they are prevented from doing so by various restrictions, rules, and procedures that make it difficult for them to serve customers as they would like. Instead of buy-in, let's talk about how you can make it possible for your employees to deliver the kind of customer experience that will result in the emotional connection we are striving for.

They Need to Understand Why

In the first place, employees will need to understand why you are proposing a change in direction with respect to customers. They need to know about the changes that are taking place in the competitive marketplace and why you see a renewed focus on customers as the route to competitive advantage and long-term success. They need to know what your strategy is and what is expected of them in the execution of that strategy, and what you are prepared to do to support them. They need to see that this is a commitment on the part of your firm and the management team; it's not something that you expect them to do while you get on with business as usual. They need to understand the rationale for the changes and where a change in their behavior will fit with the overall objective. It's important to share with employees your vision of where you want the company to be two or three years from now, especially as it relates to what customers will be saying about you.

Give Them What They Need

There is little point in telling employees what is expected of them if you do not provide them with what they need to deliver on that objective. They need the tools and resources to enable them to change how they deal with customers. Therefore, you will need to convert existing technology, systems, processes, and procedures to support the new direction of the firm. What is the point in giving contact center employees the flexibility to engage customers in conversation if those customers are already irate when they get on the line after a 20-minute wait? It makes little sense to encourage employees to have products sent across town from one store to another to meet a customer need if the receiving store is charged the transportation costs. Employees and their managers should be allowed the flexibility and freedom to do whatever is reasonable to satisfy and impress a customer.

Training, of course, will be needed. But the training should be inspirational rather that telling employees what to do. Encouraging a change in behavior is often facilitated through example. You should be prepared to provide many examples of how you want employees to handle certain situations, how to anticipate and deal with problems, how to seize opportunities to impress customers. Learning is often facilitated through storytelling, where employees share their own experiences dealing with other companies, then discuss how they felt and what they would have wished to happen. Another technique that I have used is to show employees the results of customer research and, in particular, allow them to hear the comments of customers extracted from focus groups. Learning is enhanced when they can hear comments directly from customers and then have an opportunity to discuss how they would have handled the situation.

Reinforce and Reward

The rewards to employees for changing their approach to customers should be both intrinsic and extrinsic. Managers and executives should single out for attention and communicate to employees specific examples of situations where employees treated customers especially well or dealt with a problem before it escalated into a crisis. Simply mentioning to employees that they handled a situation very well goes a long way toward confirming that they are on the right track. Sharing positive customer feedback with employees is also a means of reinforcing the kinds of behavior that you are encouraging.

But you likely will also have to change the way that employees are rewarded and compensated so as to reinforce the kinds of behavior and results you are looking for. As mentioned on several occasions, if your compensation and bonus system is tied to the achievement of short-term sales and financial results, you will have to make changes. Implementing the kind of measurement system discussed in Chapter 8 will provide you with "softer" data that you can use to demonstrate progress in implementing the customer strategy and that will serve as a reference point against which you can measure individual and team performance. In the future, you may want to tie some fairly large percentage of employee compensation to customer relationship quality. Make sure you explain to employees how such measures are calculated so that they understand them and accept their validity.

Be a Role Model

How you treat your employees must be consistent with how you want them to treat customers. There is little point to encouraging them to care deeply about customers if it is not clear that you care deeply about them as well. You cannot be encouraging flexibility toward customers while demonstrating rigidity toward employees. There is a very definite need, therefore, for your firm to have an employee strategy that runs parallel to and reinforces your customer strategy. These strategies are of necessity inextricably interlinked. This is one more reason why the human resources department must be an active player in the development and execution of the customer strategy.

Managers and executives must also play a leadership role in how they themselves deal with customers. Employees will be very quick to pick up on any sense of falseness or of paying lip service to the notion of customer relationships. Management's attitude and behavior toward customers must, therefore, reinforce at every turn the philosophy that underlies the customer strategy. As soon as employees sense that management is not fully supportive and is not behaving accordingly, the strategy is doomed to failure.

Make It Meaningful

The execution of your customer strategy depends entirely on the support it receives from your front-line employees in particular. If they perceive it as a short-term initiative, as the latest big idea from management, then it will go nowhere. Therefore, it has to be a truly meaningful experience for employees, as it must be for customers; they both must notice and experience the difference. Thus, the customer strategy must be holistic; everything that you do must fit together and lead toward the collective goal of strengthened emotional connection with customers. This can't feel like the flavor of the month or a campaign. It's not yet another "customer appreciation day," as both customers and employees see such events for precisely what they are: insincere and superficial. Don't dress it up as a contest and turn it into something frivolous; it isn't. This customer strategy represents the future of your company, and you need your employees to support and deliver it.

HOW GREAT COMPANIES GOT TO BE THAT GOOD

A couple of years ago, with the cooperation of Bob Thompson, CEO of CRMguru.com, we undertook a survey of CRMguru members to determine which companies across five industry groups—hotels, airlines, supermarkets, computers, and banks—enjoyed the strongest relationships with their customer base. Utilizing the BREI (Barnes Relationship Equity Index) methodology described in Chapter 8, we collected data from an international sample. Not surprisingly, some familiar names appeared in the lists of companies whose customer relationships were particularly strong: Publix, Kroger, and Costco among supermarkets; HSBC, Bank of America, and the Royal Bank of Canada in financial services; Dell, Hewlett-Packard, and Toshiba in computers; Accor, Marriott, and Hyatt in hotels; and Southwest, Lufthansa, and British Airways in airlines.[7] Some companies that you may expect to be on the list of top relationship performers simply had too few members rating them to allow for accurate analysis.

Our research of secondary sources, including company Web sites, speeches and writings by CEOs, and articles about the companies with high BREI scores, uncovered some common themes across the top companies in all five industries. We found that the leading companies were most likely to have or exhibit these characteristics:

- Leaders who are passionate about people
- Pride in their history and heritage
- Well-defined positioning
- Ability to establish next practices
- Genuine commitment to the well-being of their employees
- Strong commitment to social and environmental responsibility
- Strong values and an unshakable commitment to them
- Understanding how to create meaning for customers, employees, and society

Leaders Who Are Passionate about People

Typically, the companies that have very strong relationships with their customers are led by CEOs who want to make a difference, not only for their customers and their employees but in society as a whole. With their inspiring messages and their concern for the well-being of people, the founders and CEOs of many of these firms have become well-respected leaders.

HSBC group chairman Sir John Bond commented in a recent speech:

> So we believe that being successful is the primary way of fulfilling our obligations to our customers, shareholders, colleagues and the world at large. At the same time, we recognize that no company can

succeed in a failed world. So every successful company, whose suc-cess is derived from the country or society where it operates, has a responsibility to contribute to the development of that community. To give something back.[8]

George Jenkins, founder of Publix, was known for his passion for people. He believed in treating his customers and his associates right, going out of his way to help them or to show he cared. Referred to as "the Jenkins Principle," Jenkins's philosophy lives on in a company that continues to make *Fortune* magazine's list of "100 Best Companies to Work For."

The relentless pursuit of customer satisfaction at Southwest Airlines is driven from the top. Herb Kelleher, cofounder of the successful airline, is a charismatic leader whose presence is felt throughout the company. He is frequently seen walking through airports and planes showing that he cares about the quality of each customer's experience with Southwest.

CEOs who are passionate about people place special importance on their employees. They show their employees respect, and, by doing so, they win the affection of their people. They lead by example, and they inspire confidence and admiration. Barney Kroger, founder of Kroger supermarkets, said: "Success isn't measured by how much merchandise you sell. Real success is found in the development of and opportunities you provide for, the people who are selling it."[9]

Pride in Their History and Heritage

Most of the companies that ranked highest in the survey were found to have a very strong sense of who they are and where they have come from. Southwest Airlines tells its story in the "History" section of its Web site and shares the vision of its founders with the public. Dell is also proud to tell its story. An entire section on its Web site relates the history of the company. HP tells the story of its founders on its site. It reads like a popular history, creating a legend for the company. It begins with: "Following graduation as electrical engineers from Stanford University in 1934, Bill Hewlett and Dave Packard go on a two-week camping and fishing trip in the Colorado Mountains during which they become close friends . . . ."

The Bank of America's story is also inspiring and provides a good example of "living the American Dream," something the bank still stands for today. The bank was started by a poor Italian farm boy named A.P. Giannini in San Francisco at the turn of the nineteenth century. The story is so captivating that books have been written about the history of the bank.

By sharing their stories, these companies are allowing their employees and customers to become more intimately acquainted with them. Employees can feel pride while customers can more easily trust these companies, thereby coming closer to establishing a relationship with them.

Well-Defined Positioning

The top companies have strong brands and they know who their market is. In this way, they can better understand their customers and create meaning for them. They can be more than just a bank, a supermarket, a computer manufacturer, an airline, or a hotel.

As "The World's Local Bank," HSBC has positioned itself as a bank that is dedicated to outstanding customer service, implementing decisions quickly, delegating authority and accountability, high standards of personal integrity, and a multicultural approach. As a global bank that wants to be thought of as a local bank in the communities it serves, HSBC strives to cut across bureaucracy and empower its employees. In this way, it can truly be viewed by its customers as a bank that cares about them and their community.

Publix has positioned itself as a family supermarket that cares about the well-being of children. The company was named by *Child* Magazine in 2003 as one of the "Top 10 Child-Friendly Supermarkets." British Airways repositioned itself as a "Citizen of the World," catering to sophisticated "global" business passengers and investing in innovative products and processes to enhance their travel experience. Similarly, Southwest Airlines does not try to be all things to all people. The company focuses on the customer segment looking for good value for money. The airline has stayed true to its founders' vision: getting passengers to their destination on time, at low cost, and making sure they have a good time. That's the Southwest brand, and the company has consistently delivered this to its customers.

Ability to Establish Next Practices

Companies that are successful at building customer relationships are successful because they behave differently. They find creative ways to get to know their customers and to create meaning for them, and this makes them difficult to imitate. They are also focused very much on the future. They know what it will take to achieve success. They are not content to rest on current best practices; they constantly look for next practices.

Costco is a leader in service and innovation. Competitors study and imitate the company's practices. At the heart of Costco's service quality is its employees, who are paid well despite criticism from investors. But CEO Jim Sinegal dares to behave differently. As he explains, his employees "are entitled to buy homes and live in reasonably nice neighborhoods and send their children to school."[10] By treating his employees well, Sinegal creates a culture of respect. And the payoffs include lower employee turnover and high customer satisfaction scores.

Genuine Commitment to the Well-Being of Their Employees

Customer-centric companies value their employees and spend the time and money necessary for recruiting and training. They also reward their employees and make them feel important. Accor is so committed to training its employees well that it established the Academie Accor, which was the first corporate university in Europe. In addition, Accor has an international network of 150 HR managers who adapt the corporate HR policy to the local culture and laws.

Publix cares about the dignity and well-being of its employees and offers them numerous benefits and wages that are higher than the minimum. At Southwest Airlines, there is a genuine family atmosphere. The airline knows that concern and care for employees leads to concern and care for customers.

Strong Commitment to Social and Environmental Responsibility

Companies that care about people and the environment appear to win the affection of their customers. The top-ranked companies give generously and are rewarded for it. For example, Dell has a "One Dell, One Community volunteer program" and the Dell Foundation for Children.

Accor's commitment to the environment is driven from the top. Accor has an environment department with employees on five continents to provide expertise and training at every level of the business. Accor also has a Sustainable Development Purchasing Charter to ensure that its certified suppliers share its commitment to protecting people and the environment. Despite bleak times for the airline industry, Lufthansa has managed to stay committed to its causes, which include the environment. The airline has won numerous awards for its commitment to environmental protection, including being voted industry leader in the Dow Jones Sustainability Index World for 2004, a position it has held every year since 1999.

Strong Values and an Unshakable Commitment to Them

The top companies have strong values and are committed to living them; they don't simply list their values on their Web sites. HSBC uses the slogan "Living our Values" to demonstrate how its core values translate into action through its community programs, active company-sponsored employee volunteerism, corporate social responsibility, and customer care. For example, one of the company's key business values is to promote good environmental practice and sustainable development. To this end, HSBC is working with organizations such as the World Wildlife Fund and Earthwatch to improve rivers and undertake conservation projects around the world.

Dell calls its corporate philosophy "the Soul of Dell"; it espouses a dedication to its customers, to teamwork, to direct relationships, to global citizenship, and to a winning culture. The Bank of America lives its values, one of which is "inclusive meritocracy" in which the company states that it respects and values differences. Its program to support multicultural supplier development aims at helping diverse businesses expand and thrive. The values that these top companies live every day become a central part of their culture, and a strong people-focused culture is difficult to imitate.

Understanding How to Create Meaning for Customers, Employees, and Society

When a company understands how to create meaning in the lives of customers, employees, and people in general, it is one step closer to understanding how to build relationships.

Dell's Volunteers of Distinction Grant Program recognizes Dell employees worldwide who actively support their local communities. Dell understands that if its employees are proud of what the company does and stands for and if employees can become involved though volunteerism, then employees will be much more satisfied in their job, and this will be reflected in how they treat customers.

The Royal Bank of Canada (RBC) is passionate about segmentation and understanding the needs of its different segments. For example, RBC is committed to understanding the needs of students and recent graduates because the company understands that building relationships with this segment will translate into future revenue streams when these students become professionals. The bank personalizes services for this segment and goes out of its way to create meaning for them. One of its messages is "While you focus on your education we'll be there all the way, with expert advice and custom-built financial solutions, designed with you in mind." In this way, RBC is more than just a bank for these students; it is a part of their educational experience and success.

RESIST THE TEMPTATION TO TELL EVERYONE

I am intrigued that companies feel the need to tell their customers and anyone else within earshot that they are committed to customers or to excellence or to exceeding their expectations. All of this smacks of superficiality and insincerity. It suggests that you have read a management book and now see the wisdom of being excellent. The problem is that it sounds like buzzwords, and customers see right through it.

I recently was introduced to senior managers of a professional services company that states quite prominently on its Web site, in printed brochures, and in its pitch documents that it offers a new client a complete money-back guarantee if the client is not satisfied with its work after three months. Why? That simply tells me that the company is really not sure it can deliver, that there is some risk of failure here. Companies that tell me that they have a 95 percent success rate or score 8.2 on their customer satisfaction surveys run the risk of sending the opposite message: Many customers will read into such information that there is a very definite possibility of failure and of dissatisfaction. Why run the risk? You don't need to tell customers that you're good; they will notice.

PUTTING IT ALL TOGETHER

Your customer strategy cannot simply be *your* customer strategy, it must be understood and accepted throughout your company. Such understanding and acceptance likely will necessitate a great deal of change in the climate and culture of your firm. It will also require that you demonstrate your acceptance for the importance of the "softer" side of the value proposition and the validity of "softer" measures of success in order to guide the strategy. It will necessitate that you create a team commitment to the strategy and get the team on side to deliver.

Endnotes

1. Yankelovich Partners (www.yankelovich.com/thought/TL2005MarketReceptivity-Study.pdf)

2. Gerald Zaltman, *How Customers Think: Essential Insights Into the Mind of the Market* (Boston: Harvard Business School Press, 2003), p. 7.

3. Donald Sull, "Ingrained Success Breeds Failure," *Financial Times,* October 3, 2005, p. 10.

4. Roger Martin, "Seek Validity, Not Reliability," in "Breakthrough Ideas for 2005," *Harvard Business Review* 83, no. 2 (February 2005): 23–32.

5. Marc Beaujean, Johnathan Davidson, and Stacey Madge, "The 'Moment of Truth' in Customer Service," *McKinsey Quarterly,* no. 1 (2006): 63–73.

6. Teresa M. Amabile, *The Social Psychology of Creativity* (New York: Springer-Verlag, 1983).

7. For more detail on the results of this survey, see James G. Barnes and Natalie Slawinski, "Delivering Great Customer Relationships: How the Best Companies Got to Be that Good," paper presented at the fifth American Marketing Association/Academy of Marketing Management Joint Biennial Conference, Dublin, Ireland, July 2005.

8. "Managing Corporate Social Responsibilities," speech by Sir John Bond to the 38th Annual General Meeting of the Pacific Basin Economic Council, June 13, 2005.

9. www.kroger.com/careers.htm

10. http://faculty.msb.edu/murphydd/CRIC/Newsclips/COSTCO%20Nov04.doc

10

PUTTING IT ALL TOGETHER

We now bring together all of what we have been discussing throughout this book into a plan that you can implement in your business. In this chapter we outline what it takes to put your customer strategy in place. This approach is based on what I've learned from customers over many years and on customers' perceptions of how business handles itself and behaves. It is an unashamedly customer-focused approach that has as its ultimate goal the building of a strong emotional connection between your customers and your brand.

ALWAYS MOVING FORWARD

Putting your customer strategy in place will involve for your company a progression from a focus on getting the basics right to delivering emotional value. Much of what we have been illustrating in this book represents a continuum or, more correctly, a series of continua. Companies progress along a continuum from a focus on the functional to a focus on the emotional. Critically important concepts that we have addressed, including customer value, customer emotions, and customer experience, may each be viewed on a continuum.

You must understand where you stand as a company and the extent to which you are committed to moving along the continuum. You must raise the question of organizational readiness. Do you have the right frame of mind, the right understanding and commitment to move from your current view of the customer to one that will allow for the creation of that emotional connection? Is your organization prepared to put the resources behind the transformation?

The change that is implicit in becoming a truly customer-focused organization demands leadership from the top. Your firm must see this customer strategy as a solid business strategy, not as naïve or tangential to the real mission of the firm. I am certain that the reaction of some senior executives to whom I speak on the subject of a customer strategy is "This is all very well and good, but I've got a business to run here." In other words, their view is that the business is all about producing financial results, meeting quarterly budgets. Most businesspeople acknowledge that the firm is in business to provide a return to its shareholders, to make profits, to succeed and grow. And it is increasingly being acknowledged that a focus on customers represents a legitimate way to get there.

Your firm must respond to the changing realities of the marketplace and of customers and to all of the forces that are at work that make the competitive landscape different from what it was five years ago or even six months ago. This is a long-run strategy that will form a buffer against the exigencies of marketplace change. Before you embark on the process of putting your customer strategy together, your management team must demonstrate its commitment to the principles and to leading the change.

AGREEMENT TO FIRST PRINCIPLES

Before you and your management team begin to develop the details of your customer strategy, it is important that you have reached agreement on some of the basic principles that we have presented in earlier chapters. You will need to ensure that your team is fully accepting of the need for a customer strategy in your firm and that everyone is committed to developing a closer emotional connection with your customers.

We have presented and reinforced several key principles that are fundamental to the cultivation of genuine customer relationships and that form the basis for a customer strategy. Without agreement on these and acceptance of their importance, it is unlikely that you will be able to create the kind of strategy that will make a difference in how customers see your firm and in how it is able to compete.

The principles that will guide the development of your customer strategy include:

- Recognition that the "softer," emotional side of the value proposition is at least as important as the functional side.
- Acceptance that the firm must create new and different forms of value for your customers.

- Commitment to personalizing the customer connection.
- Commitment also to greater customization of the customer interaction; singling them out for special treatment.
- Acceptance of the importance of emotions and the need to appeal to customer emotions.
- Recognition of the role of concepts such as sharing and involvement in the cultivation of customer relationships.
- Utilization of the element of surprise, doing different things and doing the things you do differently.
- Commitment to exceeding the passive expectations of customers in particular, leading to surprise.
- Eventually coming to mean more to them by addressing what's relevant; becoming more than just another company.
- Commitment to helping customers to achieve things and to become more successful in their lives.
- Recognition that your company and its employees will have to behave differently in the future in their dealings with customers.

UNDERSTAND THE STRATEGY

You are developing a plan for understanding and dealing with your customers. It will be a *strategic* plan because it plots a way forward and is based on solid information. That's what being strategic means to me: that we have a very good reason for doing something and that it's backed up by incontrovertible information. Presumably we have made the case for a customer strategy, based on your company's intent to get closer to its customers and to establish a differential competitive advantage that derives from how you deal with and treat customers.

Let's talk about solid information. It is always useful at this preliminary stage of developing your customer strategy to review all of the marketing research information that your firm may have commissioned in the past few years. You should extract from a comprehensive review of that information, and any other information that pertains to your marketplace and your customer base, a detailed overview of the situation your firm is currently facing. Essentially, we need to know what is happening out there that affects your customers and, by extension, your firm.

It is of critical importance that your customer strategy lines up with higher-level strategic decisions that your firm has made. It is entirely likely that you and your management group have already addressed some important questions related to target customer segments, corporate positioning, and branding. If so, you will need to review those strategies at this stage. If not, you will need to address these higher-level issues prior to putting your customer strategy together.

Your strategy at the company level will play an important role in directing your customer strategy, in that decisions you will make with respect to how you will deal with customers must be made in the context of the corporate strategy and must be consistent with decisions you have made at these levels. The broader corporate strategy has four central components:

1. Selection of a number of segments of customers whom you can serve well and that represent an opportunity for you to excel and win their loyalty.

2. Positioning of your firm or brand in such a way that it will occupy a distinctive place in the hearts and minds of customers; you will stand for different things and will behave differently, thereby differentiating your firm from competitors.

3. Creation of superior forms and levels of value for customers; an appreciation on the part of your firm of the importance of emotional as well as functional value.

4. Acceptance of the role of your brand and what it stands for in the minds of your customers and of others.

LOOKING THROUGH THE LENS

The fundamental business strategies of segmentation, positioning, value creation, and branding represent four pillars of your customer strategy. Once you have these in place, and as each must reflect the values of your company and its acceptance of a new way of doing business, you will be equipped with a solid road map to guide the development and implementation of your customer strategy.

These four pillars provide a "lens" or a set of filters through which you can view and examine all aspects of your customer strategy as you develop it. At each stage, you will be able to hold decisions up to scrutiny and ask some very probing questions: Are we reaching and addressing the right customers if we do this? Do we really want to appeal to this group of customers? Is this the kind of value we set out to create? Will our target customers perceive it to be valuable? Does this proposal feel right for this firm? Is this who we really are? Does it reflect well on our brand?

Decisions that you will have made on these four strategic pillars will really guide you on "fit" and "feel." Does what we are thinking of doing—that event, that decor change, taking that initiative, behaving in that way, hiring that salesperson—really fit with the company we have decided to be and the customers with whom we want to deal? Does it feel right for us? Is this really who we are?

Many books and articles have been written on the four strategic pillars, reflecting the fact that there are many different ways to approach decisions on each of them. There is no single solution that fits all firms. You must approach decisions in these areas in a way that works for you and your colleagues in the context of your firm.

Identifying Segments

You cannot put in place a customer strategy unless you have a detailed understanding of the customers to whom you are directing your efforts. You must identify the principal segments that will be the object of your customer strategy. Keep the segments to a manageable number and define them as precisely as possible, using more than demographic descriptors. Suggesting that you are targeting all women aged 18 to 45 is neither realistic nor practical. You should develop detailed profiles of each of the principal segments and ensure that you have the insight needed to truly understand them. This is a critical set of decisions; everything that you do with respect to your customer strategy must be done with these customers in mind.

Positioning

Your firm will have to address the question of its positioning so as to appeal to each of the customer segments. In fact, these two decisions—what segments to address and how the firm is to be positioned—cannot be separated; they must be made concurrently. You can't decide what kind of company you want to be until you have decided to whom you want to appeal. Conversely, you can't decide on target customer segments that do not fit with the kind of company you are capable of being. These joint decisions essentially determine the desired image of your firm going forward, what the company is to be known for among its customers and prospective customers. It builds on the company's current strengths and takes into consideration the ways in which the firm can differentiate itself by addressing a broader range of customer needs.

Value

One of the central elements of your customer strategy is the creation of value for customers, with particular emphasis on the creation of emotional value. I am convinced that most managers inherently understand that an important role of the firm is to create value for customers, but that a majority of them believe that value mainly has something to do with the price being charged. It is critical to appreciate the multidimensional and complex nature of value and the fact that value is a perception on the part of customers. It is also essential for your firm to identify the forms of value to be created and enhanced. You will address your current approach to value creation and where more valuable forms of value can be created for customers. At each stage, you will be asking yourselves: Does this add value in the eyes of our customers?

Branding

Your branding is the external presentation or manifestation of your positioning. This component of your strategy addresses the question of how your company will be presented to your target segments, so as to ensure that the approach to branding is consistent with other aspects of the customer strategy. The brand must stand for something special, and this fact must guide not only communications but also corporate and individual behavior. You must live the brand in your dealings with customers.

SUPPORTING DECISIONS

Prior to the development of your customer strategy, and following the steps just outlined, you will need to address and reach agreement on four necessary, parallel, and supporting components of the strategy. It is advisable to have addressed these questions before beginning to put your strategy together. If decisions are made on these subjects early in the process, you will have in place a solid foundation for moving forward as well as the infrastructure to ensure that you will be able to measure the success of the strategy, to obtain management and employee commitment, and ensure that your company is ready to take on this challenge.

Gathering Customer Insight

How will you obtain the knowledge and insight of target customers that will allow you to craft an appropriate strategy that is grounded in customer needs?

You will need to do an assessment of current levels of customer understanding and where gaps, if any, exist that you may need to fill. Then you will almost certainly have to gather some additional insight to fill in some gaps and to ensure that you know your target customers as well as you possibly can. Spend some time with your team reviewing your need for insight and then plan how you will obtain it. You may well need to engage professional help to gather the insight you need, so you should be prepared to allocate an appropriate budget.

Measuring Progress

You will need to reach agreement on the adequacy of existing measurement tools to enable you to assess your firm's performance in implementing the new customer strategy. You will need to address the need for a combination of "hard" measures and "soft" measures that are customized to evaluate your progress in building the desired emotional connection with customers. Chances are you won't have such measures in place at the moment, so you will need to develop them and then figure out how to collect the data; again, you will likely have to work with research professionals to put your system in place. It is also a very good idea that you develop your measurement tools as you put your strategy together and *before* you start to roll it out. Then you should undertake baseline research, prior to launching the strategy. This will provide you with benchmark numbers relating to the kind of soft measures that we discussed in Chapter 8 and will provide an indication of the current quality of the emotional connection with customers and where you need to improve. You will then be able to measure your progress as you conduct follow-up customer research 6 or 12 months after implementation.

Achieving Support and Buy-in

Much of the success of the customer strategy will depend on how well it is accepted and supported within the firm. In that customer relationships are greatly influenced by the customers' interaction with your employees, it is critical that you have employee understanding, acceptance, and support for the new direction. To this end, it will be necessary to plan for briefings throughout the company and for the implementation of a training and communications program. Follow the thinking outlined in Chapter 9 and continue to reinforce the new direction as you roll out your customer strategy.

Organizational Change

As this initiative will generally mark a departure from current thinking within the firm, you need to do an assessment of organizational readiness for the change, where you stand at the moment on the continuum that marks the progression of organizational thinking from a product/sales focus to a customer relationship focus. You will need to address a number of organizational change implications. Principally, you and your management team will need to be able to assess just how committed your company is to taking on this challenge.

PROGRESSION OF THINKING AND ACTION

You will now need to consider your strategy for moving your firm along the continuum relating to each of the stages of the *drivers of customer relationships* model introduced in Chapter 2. Exhibit 10.1 shows the major components of a customer relationship strategy. We first establish the principle that there are five levels through which a company passes on its journey from being focused on "what we make or do" to being focused on building an emotional connection with customers. Part of your assessment of your company's position before you start to build your strategy should address where you stand on this progression: What is the principal focus of your company today? Where are most of your employees focused? At what stage are you in your evolution toward a solid relationship with your customers? How good is your performance at each of the five levels of this model? Have you progressed farther with some segments than with others?

Understanding the Drivers

You will need to ensure that there is understanding of the factors and tools that contribute to your progressing from the "core," with its emphasis on functional product and price elements, to an "emotional connection," where the customer is made to feel valued and appreciated. To do well at the first stage of the model, you will need to deliver high-quality products and services, something that most companies seem to be able to achieve today. With advances in technology and systems design, many companies are also getting to be very good at the second stage. As you move toward the higher levels of the model, what is needed to "deliver" to the customer becomes more complex and difficult to organize and manage. At the top two levels, success depends on how well you hire, motivate, and support your employees and on how they and your company collectively "behave" toward your customers. These are areas with which many managers are decidedly uncomfortable.

Understanding Their Expectations

In order to create an emotional link to customers, it is important that their expectations are exceeded and that they are impressed. You will need to

Exhibit 10.1 Progression of Thinking and Action Toward an Emotional Connection

Stages of Customer Relationship Building	Relationship Drivers	Customer Expectations	Value Created	Customer Emotions	Customer Experience
LEVEL 5: The emotional connection: How your firm or brand makes the customer feel	The element of surprise and emotional connection; customer is clearly valued and feels truly appreciated	Expectations are generally passive; not expecting to be surprised or impressed	High-order value; customer is impressed and grateful; feels unique; problems are solved, needs addressed	High-order positive emotions: love, pride, etc.; creates meaning; reduces negatives like disgust, humiliation, anger	Transcends what the firm typically does; addresses what it contributes to; makes possible
LEVEL 4: Getting to know us: Interpersonal connection; where the customer meets our people; face-to-face or through technology	The quality and behavior of our people; how they deal with and treat the customer; the interaction or experience	Employees will be helpful, pleasant, courteous, civil, available, knowledgeable	More personal forms of value, individualized, respect; employees are caring and empathetic	People-based emotions like trust, comfort, friendliness, sense of community, association; reduce frustration, embarrassment, neglect	Employees important in creating positive experience, customization, personalization, ambiance, facilitation
LEVEL 3: Getting it right: Delivering on promises; meeting commitments; accuracy	Delivery is on-time; service is prompt; systems, procedures, and processes work as they should	The firm will meet its commitments; they will generally get things right; accuracy	Reliability; be there when needed; errors are minimized; superior technical service	Satisfaction, relief; peace of mind; reduce anxiety, disappointment, regret	Everything goes according to plan; no surprises; service delivered as promised
LEVEL 2: Backup support: Systems and processes that enhance and support the core	Access and convenience; technology-based systems and procedures; delivery, scheduling,	Product and service will be conveniently available; firm will have necessary systems and processes in place	Access and convenience; make it easy to deal with us; choice and selection	Generally pleased at availability of processes; not particularly impressed unless they are unavailable	Interaction often with technology; impersonal, emphasis on being easy to do business with; in the zone
LEVEL 1: The core: The essence of what the company offers; what it makes or sells, what it does	Functional product and service quality	The core will work; quality is acceptable; it won't fail	Product quality; value for money; good product for the price charged	Not much emotion involved; very transactional; minimize annoyance, irritation, worry	Very basic; very little interaction may be involved; product and service availability

179

ensure that there is an understanding of how the firm progresses through the five stages from where customers expect relatively little, to where you are exceeding expectations that customers do not even realize they have— the element of surprise. This point is of critical importance in the development of your customer strategy. If you are going to create a meaningful difference in the minds of your customers between you and your competitors, you must set out to exceed passive expectations. Everyone is out to minimally exceed obvious expectations; you must seize the opportunity to create surprise by doing unexpected things, not by doing better the things you already do.

Creating Meaningful Value

There must also be an appreciation among your management team and employees for the fact that value can be created at each level of the customer relationships model and that special forms of value must be created in order to establish an emotional connection with the customer. As you progress through the stages of relationship building, you must be creating more valuable forms of value. You will also progress from a focus on the creation of functional value, to a focus on emotional value. The top stages of the model are all about the interpersonal and emotional connection with customers. These involve higher-order forms of value, forms that many firms have not consciously addressed.

Understanding Emotions

The establishment of a close connection with customers demands an understanding of the role of emotions in building relationships. There exists a hierarchy of emotions, and you must strive to create high-level positive emotions and reduce or eliminate high-level negative emotions. Examine where you are currently creating various emotions in your interaction with customers. Most transactions with customers are completed with very little emotional content. At best, nothing important goes wrong, and at worst, low-intensity emotions such as annoyance or disappointment are evoked, as when customers can't get served quickly or when an item is out of stock. But there is ample evidence that customers feel higher-intensity negative emotions on a fairly regular basis—every customer has many horror stories that caused him or her to walk away. The challenge is to understand the role of higher-intensity positive emotions in cementing strong customer relationships and then focusing on how your company can create them with some degree of consistency.

Creating Memorable Experiences

All aspects of your firm's interaction with customers contribute to the creation of emotional responses and ultimately to the kind of relationship you have with them. You will need to address all details of the customer experience in its various forms, realizing that most interactions with customers are decidedly unmemorable. Your challenge in addressing the role of the customer experience is twofold. First, you should appreciate that every interaction with a customer should be thought of as an experience that can be improved on. They really are "moments of truth" where things can go surprisingly right or disastrously wrong. Second, your management team and employees must realize that the customer experience and your responsibility do not end when the customer walks out the door. You must not only address the fact that your employees are instrumental in creating positive customer experiences and that the experience extends to the customer's enjoyment of the product or service in use. The real challenge and, therefore, the real opportunity exists in focusing on the kinds of experiences that you can create or facilitate for your customers.

Implementation: Putting the Building Blocks in Place

At this point, you have made strategic decisions relating to target customer segments, positioning, branding, and value creation. You have addressed fundamental concepts of relationship building, including customer expectations, emotions, and experiences. We now revisit the 12 building blocks of customer relationships first introduced in Chapter 4, as these represent the tools that you can use to deliver on your strategy. You and your employees should be constantly on the lookout for opportunities to implement these. Build them into your interaction with your customers. Some are spontaneous, while others require more formal planning.

We will illustrate how some very successful firms are making use of these concepts and will give you some ideas of how you can implement them within your firm. Learn from those that are doing it well. You also know of companies with which you have had experience that do these things routinely with great results. Think of them, how they behave and how they make you feel, and then set out to emulate them.

1. **Demonstrate that you appreciate their business.** The secret here is to be genuine. Lots of companies thank their customers for their business but few sound as if they really mean it. The appropriately named hospitality industry—mainly the larger hotel chains, such

as Four Seasons, Ritz-Carlton, and Westin—make great use of their frequent-guest information systems to recognize returning guests and to welcome them. Contrast this with the plastic "thank you for shopping at _____" that characterizes much of retail.

Let's distinguish between showing appreciation and rewarding customers. You don't need to establish a "loyalty program," in part because this is 20-year-old thinking and such programs don't really create loyalty, anyway. You don't have to give things away to your truly loyal customers. Just treat them special.

2. **Earn their trust; be consistent, dependable, and reliable.** Many of the best companies have built entirely deserved reputations for being totally reliable—you can always count on them to live up to their explicit and implicit promises. Names like Disney, McDonald's, Dell, and Tesco come to mind. Two companies that I have always found to deliver consistently impressive customer experiences are Federal Express and Kinko's. It came as no surprise to me when FedEx acquired Kinko's. This was a cultural fit as well as a logical extension of the FedEx business model.

   Nothing confuses and irritates customers more than inconsistency. If you have some employees interpreting policy one way and others another way, customer frustration will result. If customers decide that they can no longer count on you to deliver on time or to have important items in stock, they will find someone who does.

3. **Single them out for attention, personalize, and customize.** Again, armed with sophisticated database technology, many of the major banks do a solid job of recognizing the value of customers and of paying individualized attention to them. Royal Bank of Canada's "First" advertising campaign places the interests of customers ahead of the bank's, an attitude that seems to pervade the organization. Lands' End is a great example of a company that uses technology to customize the customer experience—check out the "Virtual Model" on its Web site and build yourself an outfit.

   The opposite of paying attention is to ignore customers. Many with whom I have talked have provided numerous examples of situations where they have walked out of businesses because no one paid them any attention—more "almost customers." Personalize the interaction by asking pertinent questions; show you are genuinely interested in solving their problems and in contributing to their success.

4. **Partner with them, help them achieve and accomplish.** This step is all about helping customers do well the things they need to do,

so that they can be happy or even proud of what they have been able to accomplish. We're not talking about climbing Everest or winning Olympic gold, but rather the things that make small life events special. The Home Depot will help its customers learn how to lay ceramic tile, build a tree house, or hang wallpaper. The Canadian specialty chain Running Room helps its customers run their first 10k race or half-marathon by offering running clinics and organizing groups who do training runs together. UPS manages the logistics of computer repair for Toshiba, actually looking after the shipping, repair, and return of computers to Toshiba's customers.

There are many ways that your firm can help your customers accomplish things, to be successful at what they have set out to do. This may mean offering classes or providing CDs with detailed step-by-step instructions. If you have provided them with the knowledge and skills, and have thereby contributed to their being able to pull it off, guess where they'll come to buy what they need and where they'll send their friends?

5. **Create customer involvement, build communities.** Anything that allows the customer to participate actively in creating something or in accomplishing a goal builds involvement, for which customers can take credit. The Home Depot and Running Room examples apply here as well, as both involve customers actually going to their stores to participate.

Customization is closely related to involvement because customers create something unique that they actually designed or built. IKEA is a wonderful example because its customers actually assemble the furniture and feel a sense of accomplishment as a result. Jones Soda allows customers to design their own labels; Dell allows its customers to select their own components; and Build-a-Bear Workshop allows Sarah to create her very own teddy bear, unlike anyone else's.

You can get your customers much more involved with you in creating things. From book clubs, to cooking classes, to pruning lessons, to how-to-drive-safely-in-winter classes for young drivers, virtually any business can develop creative ideas to add to its role in helping customers get things done. Also, every time you have a group of customers together, you are creating a community with a connection to your firm. Cultivate it, build alumni events, and keep them together. They will be your best ambassadors.

6. **Establish effective two-way communications.** Companies must look at communications as a fundamentally important component of relationship building. If customers never hear from you, or can't reach you, the relationship has little possibility of developing. Two-way communications is critical, but the communication must be relevant. If not, it is deemed to be junk or spam. Some of the major international consulting firms, including McKinsey, Mercer Management, and Booz Allen Hamilton, have established management journals that they make available to clients and other readers online, thereby sending a message to their clients that they want to help them keep informed.

Unfortunately, much of what customers receive from firms is not considered to be particularly useful, geared as it typically is to trying to persuade customers to buy more things. Ideally, communications should be useful and pertinent to things that the customer needs to accomplish. Consider what you could be sending your customers that they will find useful and that will position your firm as their partner in getting certain things done.

Communications must also be effective with other key groups, including employees and channel partners. They are integral components of your customer focus. If they feel left out, they will not be committed to executing the strategy as you need them to do. One particularly disgruntled channel partner asked, "How come I have to hear about it from my customers?"

7. **Share things with your customers.** What do you and your customers have in common? Companies that can demonstrate to their customers that they have the same interests and values have an advantage in building a connection. A sense of community is often implicit in sharing in that we share things with members of a community to which we belong. Sharing, membership, community, and belonging are all aspects of a feeling of closeness. Some companies are very successful at creating that closeness. BB&T is a bank that has squarely positioned itself as a community bank and created a small-bank feel, even though it is a $100 billion company.

Also, look for opportunities to actually share more than memories or values with customers, to send them new information that pertains to better use of your product or to share knowledge with them about new and better ways to get certain things done.

8. **Remind them of things.** Customers often associate certain brands with special occasions or with good times. Some companies have

effectively used music that strikes a chord with customers, especially the music of their youth. Some brands have woven themselves into the fabric of a society over time and have been an integral part of the lives of their customers for many years. Tim Hortons has accomplished this in Canada by never wavering from its position and by using real-life examples provided by customers as a basis for much of its television advertising.

9. **Associate with what's central in their lives.** Many companies have gotten closer to their customers by connecting with things that clearly mean something to them. Estee Lauder's support for breast cancer research; the Dove Self-Esteem Fund, which is part of Unilever's campaign to help women and girls celebrate their individual beauty; Publix Supermarkets' partnership with Upromise to enable their customers to save for their children's college education are all great examples of companies that demonstrate commitment to the things that are central to the lives of their customers.

   You can also "infiltrate" the lives of your customers at a more local level by becoming involved with the things that are important to them and their families. This requires that you know a lot about what customers are interested in and passionate about so that you can tailor events and sponsorships appropriately.

10. **Piggyback on their relationships with others.** Your customers have existing relationships with other brands, with sports and entertainment personalities, with various activities such as gardening, jogging, old movies, and so on. Information concerning these relationships should be critical in determining how you make decisions relating to sponsorships, spokespersons, and partnerships. The key word here is "fit." You must associate with things that are right for your firm or brand. Before you decide to spend money on sponsorships, you should determine whether the event or personality involved really means something special to your target segments. If not, pass on the opportunity. Don't sponsor something just because you are really keen on it, and don't decide to partner with another firm on a promotion just because you and its CEO play golf together.

11. **Get rid of irritants and stupid rules.** Customer interactions are full of irritants that may, in and of themselves, not be deal breakers but that constantly nag at customers and certainly make them more receptive to competitive overtures. Wireless telephone customers are frustrated by some carriers' refusal to allow them to change the

terms of their contracts, even when they want to upgrade their service and would actually be spending more monthly with the company. Such irritants and stupid rules send a loud message to customers that the company really isn't interested in them. Remember the single-ply factor.

12. **Surprise them every now and then.** We end with the element of surprise; a component of your strategy that has the greatest potential to impress customers and to build an emotional connection. It sends the message that you have noticed something and are prepared to rise to the occasion. Be the Air Canada flight attendant who offers the shivering 13-year-old her own sweater when there are no blankets to be found. Be the waiter in the Mexican restaurant who brings complimentary sangria for regular guests because they are such great customers. Repair the small tear in the jacket when it's sent in for dry cleaning. Such surprises are not scripted and mean that much more to customers because of that.

IMPLICATIONS FOR OTHER AREAS

We have made the point at several stages in the development of your customer strategy that this new direction for your firm is an all-encompassing one. It is not an assignment that you hand to a "customer strategy manager" to develop and implement. Nor is it a project that you engage a consultant to do on your behalf. It demands a commitment from the top, and it will have an impact on the entire company. As you develop the strategy and roll it out, it will be obvious that no part of your company will be untouched by the new culture.

You will need to address the implications of the new customer strategy for other components of the marketing mix or value proposition and for other divisions and areas within the company. You will have to be constantly asking yourself, "What does this change mean for the kinds of people we hire, how we train them, the telephone system, the design of our Web site, how we advertise, how we set prices?" Everything that you do as a company must be completely consistent with the new customer focus.

If the consistency or "fit" is missing, your customers will be confused; they will hear you saying one thing and doing another, or they will experience great performance in some areas and not in others. Your employees will be frustrated if they hear you espousing the commitment of the company to a customer focus, but refusing to put resources behind the commitment or failing to ensure that customers are treated well at every interaction.

Specifically, you will need to consider what your new customer-relationships-focused culture means for your company in each of these areas:

- Product
- Processes/technology/rules
- Customer service/interaction
- People
- Communications
- Communities/events/sponsorships
- Sales and distribution channels
- Pricing

Product

What new products and variations on products should you consider introducing that will add value for customers? As we have been developing your customer strategy, we have placed considerable emphasis on the creation of higher-order forms of value and on high-intensity emotions. Our focus has been mainly on the higher stages of our *drivers of customer relationships* model. That is not to say that the lower levels are unimportant. In fact, it must be emphasized that unless these levels are addressed adequately, there is little hope that your company will be able to develop the kinds of emotion-based relationships that we are striving for. It is critical that you offer products and services that meet customer expectations. If customers experience failure with any degree of regularity at this level, you will never build that emotional connection.

You should address the broader question of your value proposition: What products and services should be added or modified? Take the broadest possible view of your value proposition and constantly be looking for new and different ways to impress customers. Don't ever assume that what you offer is good enough.

Processes/Technology/Rules

Address the question of how you deal with customers, the systems and processes that are in place between your firm and its customers. How can these be made more friendly, integrated, and support the effort to strengthen the relationship? It is impossible to deliver great customer experiences if unfriendly technology gets in the way, or if you make your customers jump through several hoops to get anything done.

While we have observed that the very important concept of customer experience should be viewed as more than being easy to deal with, if you are *not* easy to deal with, again you have little hope of establishing anything approaching a relationship. I hear often from customers that they give up trying to deal with some companies because they simply can't get anyone's attention or they encounter too many barriers. You really do have to make it easier for them.

Customer Service/Interaction

How do your firm and its employees interact with your customers? What kind of experience is it for them? How can you make it easier, more pleasant, productive, and so forth? How do you handle them, treat them, and deal with them? This is an area of critical importance as your employees are the first line of contact with your firm. Increasingly, of course, customer service is being delivered through technology; customers are being asked to deliver their own service. Therefore, the quality of service being provided overlaps the process and technology area that we have just discussed and the area of human resources, which follows.

Many companies have established "customer service" departments that are largely responsible for operating customer contact centers, for fielding customer calls and e-mails, and for handling enquiries and complaints. I see two possible problems in having such departments in place. The first is the possibility that customer service is seen as only the responsibility of these departments. Second, there is a danger of a silo mentality taking shape in which customer service is seen to be separate from marketing, sales, and other departments of the firm. This should not happen, as interacting with and serving customers are fundamental responsibilities of all employees and an essential foundation for the establishment of customer relationships.

People

As we have observed at many points throughout this book, your employees are critical to establishing a customer-focused culture in your firm and for creating the emotional connection. You must address the question of whom you hire and how they are trained, motivated, compensated, and evaluated. All of these decisions must be made such that they are completely consistent with the direction in which you are moving your company. The people who represent your firm in its dealings with its customers are critical to the development of solid relationships.

The human resources implications of a move toward a greater focus on customers are tremendous. That is why you will have to ensure that representatives of your human resources department are present and deeply involved throughout the process of developing and rolling out your customer strategy. If you do not have a formal human resources function within your firm, you may wish to engage an advisor to provide guidance on people matters. At the very least, you must keep this area at the forefront of your thinking at all times.

Communications

All communication from the firm, both external and internal, should speak to the new commitment to customers, to your positioning and brand values. A relationship-focused communications program directed to customers and employees should be developed and implemented. It is very confusing to and frustrating for customers to see and hear advertising from firms that emphasizes their commitment to excellence or superior service or exceeding expectations, only to experience something quite different.

You will also have to look at communications in its broadest sense. The kinds of communications that your customers receive from you, the frequency and tone of those communications all must be reviewed in the context of your new positioning vis-à-vis the customer. This has implications for your advertising agency, for campaign management, for database management, and for seemingly peripheral areas such as store decor and how your employees are dressed. Everything you do communicates, and you must be constantly asking whether you are sending the right messages and whether it feels right for your company.

Communities/Events/Sponsorships

How your firm conducts itself and is presented as part of a wider community is also critical to the success of the customer strategy. Your company must be involved in things that are important to and meaningful for your customers. The events, sponsorships, and partnerships in which you engage must be seen to be appropriate by your target customers. The concept of "fit" applies here as well. What you do in these important areas must fit with the values that you share with your target customers, with the kind of company they want you to be.

There are two applications of the very important concept of "communities" that you will need to consider. The first relates to being a supportive part of the communities in which your company operates and in which your target customers live and do business. Communities should not be defined in a narrow geographic sense, as your customers are part of groups to which they feel particularly close; there are communities of young mothers, of triathletes, and of bridge players.

There are also communities that you might want to create so as to bring customers closer to your firm. These might involve you in forming hiking clubs, book launches, teddy bears' picnics, poetry readings, or how-to-get-your-garden-ready-for-winter seminars. All tap into shared interests of your customers and help them meet like-minded people, all under your sponsorship.

Sales and Distribution Channels

There are questions to be addressed relating to the most effective sales and distribution channel to serve your customers. You will need to address how that channel will look in the future in order to be consistent with the new approach to the customer. How you get your products and services to customers will affect their impression of your firm and of your commitment to them. Decisions relating to channel structure and the kinds of partners you need would appear to affect mainly the more functional levels of the customer relationship model. This is indeed the case, as the distribution channel will obviously affect access, availability, and convenience. But choice of channel partners and distributors is similar to employee selection in that these firms will be perceived by customers as your representatives and your front line.

Pricing

Finally, there are a number of issues relating to pricing that will have to be addressed as the customer strategy is developed. Focus on price will depend on decisions taken with respect to segmentation and positioning. When discussing what prices to set, it is always important to keep one eye firmly focused on value. Discuss pricing in the context of your value proposition and ask yourself what it is you are offering your customers and what they are likely to be prepared to pay for it. If you are seen by customers to be selling a commodity that is no better than anyone else's, then you have little choice but to be a price follower. But one of the principal outcomes of the development of a customer strategy is a decommoditization effect. In other words, you have set out to create a clear difference between you and your competitors, to be seen to be adding value in ways that they cannot match. If you are successful, this takes the customer's eye off price and allows you to price differently than you would have done previously. There is a price premium associated with an effective customer strategy.

OVER TO YOU!

To develop and implement a successful customer strategy demands leadership, commitment, and consistency. This is not a short-term project that can be delegated to middle managers to get done. There must be an organization-wide commitment to turning your company into a truly customer-focused firm. Everything that you and your employees do and every interaction with a customer must be considered important in leading to an emotional connection.

People are emotional beings; companies typically are not. It does not come naturally to many organizations to adopt this view of the customer. You will have to find a balance between the hard side and the soft. In an environment that is often dominated by left-brain thinking, you will need to establish the legitimacy of the softer view of the world. You may find the culture change that is necessary to be a daunting task. Surround yourself with people who share your values and commitment, and make sure that a customer-focused view prevails. You have to lead by example.

Pay attention to the little things. Your customers notice things that you and your employees may miss, and these things have the potential to drive customers away. Be proactive. Constantly look for ways to impress customers by doing the unexpected, by adding a "nice touch." Customer expectations are not that difficult to exceed, especially if your employees are thinking laterally. Encourage creativity. Give your employees the authority to bend rules and to do some different things to create emotional value. The payback will come through a long-term connection with your customers that your competitors will find impossible to duplicate. They will bring not only their business to you, but that of their friends and associates.

But this all begins with your decision to wear your customer hat to work every day!

Appendix

Customer Strategy Template

The development of your customer strategy begins with a commitment by the management team and those who are working on the development of strategy to certain principles.

- *Background and Overview*
  You will begin by confirming the need in your company for a customer strategy: how it can assist in your gaining a competitive advantage and in providing the basis for stability and growth for your company. You will need to prepare an overview of what's going on in the competitive landscape and review existing customer research.

- *First Principles, Rationale*
  You and your colleagues will need to reinforce your commitment to strategic principles, including a shared understanding of what it means to be strategic. You should agree why a customer focus is needed and on the need to build an emotional connection with customers.

- *Being Strategic*
  This will be a strategic plan in that it plots a way forward. It will be based on solid information on customers and the marketplace, and a commitment to a strategic approach.

An effective customer strategy must be developed in a way that is entirely consistent with and that follows from strategic decisions taken in the broader context of the firm. These components of the customer strategy will provide a lens through which all proposed changes and initiatives should be viewed.

Step 1. Looking through the lens

Step 2. Identifying segments

Step 3. Positioning

Step 4. Value

Step 5. Branding: values, characteristics, personality

Prior to the development of the customer strategy, and following the five steps just outlined, you will need to address and reach agreement on four necessary, parallel, and supporting components of the strategy.

1. Gathering of customer insight
2. Measurement of progress
3. Achieving support and buy-in
4. Organizational change

You will now need to consider the strategy for moving along the continuum relating to each of the stages of the *drivers of customer relationships* model and the critical dimensions of relationship building.

- Understanding the drivers
- Understanding customer expectations
- Value creation
- Understanding customer emotions
- Creating positive customer experiences

You now progress to the implementation stage where you deal with the building blocks of the customer strategy—what you plan to do in each of these areas. You will identify action items, establish priorities, identify quick wins, assign responsibility, and determine time and budget implications.

- Demonstrating that you appreciate the customers' business
- Earning their trust by being consistent, dependable, and reliable
- Singling them out for attention; personalizing and customizing the experience
- Partnering with them; helping them achieve and accomplish things
- Creating a sense of involvement; establishing customer communities
- Establishing effective two-way communications
- Sharing things with customers; showing you have things in common
- Reminding them of pleasant and important things
- Associating with what's most important in their lives
- Piggybacking on their relationships with others
- Getting rid of irritants and stupid rules
- Surprising them every now and then

Then you will need to address the implications of the new customer strategy for other components of the marketing mix or value proposition and for other divisions and areas within the company. Specifically, you will need to address these implications:

- Product
- Processes/technology
- Customer service/interaction
- People
- Communications
- Communities, events, sponsorships
- Sales and distribution channel
- Pricing

INDEX